Ideologies in Action

Ideologies in Action: Morphological Adaptation and Political Ideas explores how political ideas move across geographical, social and chronological boundaries.

Focusing on North American and European case studies ranging from populist tax revolts through parenting advice manuals to online learning environments, the contributors propose new methods for understanding how political entrepreneurs, intellectuals and ordinary citizens deploy and redefine ideologies. All of these groups are consumers of ideology, drawing on pre-existing, transnational ideological concepts and narratives in order to make sense of the world. They are also all producers of ideology, adapting and reconfiguring ideological material to support their own political aims, desires and policy objectives. In doing so, they combine common conceptual elements – interpretations of freedom, order, national identity, democracy, community or equality – with sentiments and imaginations deeply embedded in cultural and social practice. To render these ideological practices intelligible, the contributors to this volume blend conceptual morphology, which emphasizes how meaning emerges in and through connections between political ideas, with close readings of the vernacular and experiential dimensions of ideologies in action.

This book offers new insights into how ideologies in varied social and political settings can be decoded, and challenges hierarchical distinctions between ideological 'producers' and 'consumers'. The chapters in this book were originally published as a special issue of the *Journal of Political Ideologies*.

Mathew Humphrey is Professor of Political Theory at the University of Nottingham, UK, and co-Director of the Centre for the Study of Political Ideologies. His books include *Ecological Politics and Democratic Theory* and *Authenticity: The Cultural History of a Political Concept*.

David Laycock is Professor of Political Science at Simon Fraser University, Canada. His books include *The New Right and Democracy in Canada* and *Political Ideology in Parties, Policy and Civil Society: Interdisciplinary Insights*.

Maiken Umbach is Professor of Modern History at the University of Nottingham, UK. Her books include *Private Life and Privacy in Nazi Germany, Photography, Migration, and Identity: A German-Jewish-American Story* and *Authenticity: The Cultural History of a Political Concept*.

Ideologies in Action

Morphological Adaptation and Political Ideas

Edited by
**Mathew Humphrey, David Laycock
and Maiken Umbach**

LONDON AND NEW YORK

First published 2020
by Routledge
2 Park Square, Milton Park, Abingdon, Oxon, OX14 4RN

and by Routledge
52 Vanderbilt Avenue, New York, NY 10017

Routledge is an imprint of the Taylor & Francis Group, an informa business

© 2020 Taylor & Francis

All rights reserved. No part of this book may be reprinted or reproduced or utilised
in any form or by any electronic, mechanical, or other means, now known or
hereafter invented, including photocopying and recording, or in any information
storage or retrieval system, without permission in writing from the publishers.

Trademark notice: Product or corporate names may be trademarks or registered trademarks,
and are used only for identification and explanation without intent to infringe.

British Library Cataloguing in Publication Data
A catalogue record for this book is available from the British Library

ISBN13: 978-0-367-49605-0

Typeset in Minion
by Newgen Publishing UK

Publisher's Note
The publisher accepts responsibility for any inconsistencies that may have arisen during
the conversion of this book from journal articles to book chapters, namely the inclusion
of journal terminology.

Disclaimer
Every effort has been made to contact copyright holders for their permission to reprint
material in this book. The publishers would be grateful to hear from any copyright holder
who is not here acknowledged and will undertake to rectify any errors or omissions in future
editions of this book.

Contents

Citation Information		vi
Notes on Contributors		viii

Introduction 1
Mathew Humphrey, David Laycock and Maiken Umbach

1 The political is personal: an analysis of crowd-sourced political ideas and
images from a Massive Open Online Course 9
Mathew Humphrey, Maiken Umbach and Zeynep Clulow

2 Cross-border influences or parallel developments? A process-tracing
approach to the development of social conservatism in Canada and the US 27
Jim Farney

3 Tax revolts, direct democracy and representation: populist politics in
the US and Canada 46
David Laycock

4 Inventing America, *again* 70
Howard Brick

5 Democratic babies? Françoise Dolto, Benjamin Spock and the ideology
of post-war parenting advice 89
Richard Bates

Index 108

Citation Information

The chapters in this book were originally published in the *Journal of Political Ideologies*, volume 24, issue 2 (April 2019). When citing this material, please use the original page numbering for each article, as follows:

Introduction

Mathew Humphrey, David Laycock and Maiken Umbach
Journal of Political Ideologies, volume 24, issue 2 (April 2019), pp. 113–120

Chapter 1

The political is personal: an analysis of crowd-sourced political ideas and images from a Massive Open Online Course
Mathew Humphrey, Maiken Umbach and Zeynep Clulow
Journal of Political Ideologies, volume 24, issue 2 (April 2019), pp. 121–138

Chapter 2

Cross-border influences or parallel developments? A process-tracing approach to the development of social conservatism in Canada and the US
Jim Farney
Journal of Political Ideologies, volume 24, issue 2 (April 2019), pp. 139–157

Chapter 3

Tax revolts, direct democracy and representation: populist politics in the US and Canada
David Laycock
Journal of Political Ideologies, volume 24, issue 2 (April 2019), pp. 158–181

Chapter 4

Inventing America, again
Howard Brick
Journal of Political Ideologies, volume 24, issue 2 (April 2019), pp. 182–200

Chapter 5

Democratic babies? Françoise Dolto, Benjamin Spock and the ideology of post-war parenting advice
Richard Bates
Journal of Political Ideologies, volume 24, issue 2 (April 2019), pp. 201–219

For any permission-related enquiries please visit:
www.tandfonline.com/page/help/permissions

Notes on Contributors

Richard Bates, Department of History, University of Nottingham, UK

Howard Brick, History Department, University of Michigan, USA

Zeynep Clulow, Energy Policy Research Group, University of Cambridge, UK

Jim Farney, Department of Politics and International Studies, University of Regina, Canada

Mathew Humphrey, School of Politics and International Relations, University of Nottingham, UK

David Laycock, Department of Political Science, Simon Fraser University, Canada

Maiken Umbach, Department of History, University of Nottingham, UK

Introduction

Mathew Humphrey, David Laycock and Maiken Umbach

ABSTRACT

This article argues for the analysis of the flow of ideological discourse through society within and across three distinct but interrelated levels: (1) the canonically defined, or macro level, (2) the intermediate or meso level of competitive political appeals, political relevant public discourse and cultural criticism, and (3) the everyday or micro level of conceptual use by non-experts. This differentiation among levels of ideological action and influence helps us to clarify the objects and appropriate methods of ideological analysis. Methods applied in specific cases must facilitate an effective focus on phenomena on one of these levels while still allowing recognition of the complex forms of direct and indirect conceptual influence and connection between the levels. The article also serves as an introduction to the volume, giving a brief account of the analysis and argument of each contribution.

Issue purposes and theoretical orientation

This special issue focuses on understanding how political entrepreneurs, intellectuals and ordinary citizens draw on global discursive repertoires when staking out their distinctive ideological claims. All of these groups are simultaneously consumers of ideology, drawing on pre-existing ideological concepts and narratives in order to make sense of the world, and producers of ideology, adapting, reconfiguring and developing new ideological material to support their own political aims, objectives and desires. Our contributors draw on a range of social science and humanities theoretical and interpretive perspectives[1] to examine how common conceptual elements – an imagination of freedom, order, national identity, community or equality – are deployed in a variety of British, North American and European settings. They show how these elements are activated, rearticulated, recombined, framed, 'naturalized' and located in specific political discourses and intellectual traditions for sometimes precise and sometimes rather open-ended ideological purposes.

The papers in this issue were initially presented at a workshop at Simon Fraser University, in Burnaby, British Columbia, on 4–5 July 2016. Funding for the workshop was provided by the Department of Political Science and the Faculty of Arts and Social Sciences, SFU; by the Centre for the Study of Political Ideologies, and the School of Politics and International Relations, at the University of Nottingham; and by a Connections Programme grant from the Social Sciences and Humanities Research Council of Canada.

The core features of a widely shared repertoire of ideological building blocks or imaginaries developing into identifiable ideological patterns emerged in the 19th century. In contemporary politics, they are given context-specific meanings by political actors, in different geographical and political situations, responding to new cultural, historical and institutional settings. Contributors to this special issue demonstrate the value of developing more analytically effective tools for understanding the substantive content, the processes and the often surprisingly distinctive effects, of ideological innovation. This innovation is marked by the adaptation and recycling of ideas across time and space, as well as variations in levels of ideological activity and conceptual specificity, as political discourses are re-purposed and re-imagined by widely varied actors with different objectives.

People use political ideas to interpret the world around them, to account for their own position in it and to form new ideas in the process of arguing about them. Ideas shape political behaviour in ways that cannot be reduced to objective interests or identities, such as class or gender. This became very obvious in 2016, when three major political events – the US election of Donald Trump, the UK 'Brexit' referendum and the Austrian presidential elections – produced outcomes that defied expert expectations.[2] It appears that, in spite of an ever-increasing capacity to analyse 'big data', professional pollsters and political analysts are sometimes unable to account for, much less predict, the political views of ordinary people or the political appeals to which they are attracted. The political choices people make at the ballot box do not always correspond in predictable ways to particular milieus. Citizens' ideas motivate political choices: not just ideas about their own identity, but also about the society they wish to live in, and the political visions they wish to see realized.

And yet, such ideas are rarely analysed by scholars of political thought. Some approaches (such as the Cambridge School's) have emphasized the role of contexts in shaping iconic political texts.[3] Agency within those contexts has remained rather diffuse, however. Anonymous entities, such as economic conditions, cultural conventions and discursive structures are portrayed as shaping major paradigms of political thought, while ordinary people's political ideas are reduced to expressions of interests or emotions.[4] Others have approached the problem through the lens of political psychology.[5] Studies in this field have examined how individuals process political information, using heuristics and other shortcuts to arrive at conclusions. However, while these studies may distinguish broadly 'conservative' and 'liberal' positions, they do not analyse the actual ideas that people hold in any detail. The emphasis in such analyses is on the process of political reasoning, and not, generally, on the content of the beliefs held.[6]

Another approach to understanding everyday political ideas has drawn on the concept of ideology. Ideology seems better suited to capturing the emotional and imaginative dynamics of vernacular political thinking than the rarefied practice of 'political thought'. And yet, the term ideology can easily impede our understanding of the role of political ideas beyond the elites as much as it can draw attention to their import. To date, the analysis of ideology has mostly been conducted relying on strong but problematic a priori assumptions. Much analysis of ideology either builds on the work of Marx and Engels to present ideology as entailing a form of 'voluntary servitude'[7] to, and false consciousness[8] about, capitalist socio-economic relations,[9] or treats ideologies as an 'Other' to clear-headed political thinking, and associating ideologies with inflexible doctrine and (state) power.[10] Both broad approaches view the phenomena of grassroots political thinking through a pejorative lens, which adds little to our incentive or ability to understand it.

A more fruitful approach for understanding the role of political ideas in everyday life is a relatively recent development in ideology analysis, which uses methods such as conceptual morphology and a notion of 'decontestation' to uncover ideas that are embedded within political and cultural practices.[11] In a parallel development in the field of conceptual history, scholars have located political ideas in broad semantic fields that are co-produced by many actors, and that metamorphose over time.[12] Such work draws on a much broader source base than the writings of 'great thinkers' to explore political ideas as rooted in, and part of, political practice. Relevant evidence includes political speeches, party political programmes and pamphlets and a wide spectrum of political commentary and cultural critique in the public sphere. The development of the methods and techniques of discourse analysis with respect to these articles of evidence has produced a sophisticated and expanding body of theory in both political science, broadly conceived, and historical analysis.[13]

Such sources are less elevated than the works of iconic philosophers, but are nevertheless produced predominantly by professionals: politicians, speech writers, spin doctors, journalists, culture critics, think tank employees and academics who double as 'public intellectuals'. As articles in this issue by Brick, Bates, Farney and Laycock demonstrate, subjecting the ideological content of such products to conceptual analysis allows for a better appreciation of how ideas flow through daily political life. This flow is both in the direction of such intermediate sources' offerings to citizens, and from foundational texts that define or influentially modify ideological traditions.

Stepping away from the public terrain of ideas self-consciously marshalled for political – if not always partisan – combat, we can also explore the interpenetration of politics with lived experience and a sense of self, which form important dimensions of political thinking at the micro- or grassroots level. Existing work has treated subjectivity mostly as a product of ideology, but ascribed little explanatory power to it.

Understanding the flow of ideological discourse through society, and the translation of political concepts from theoretical articulation to the domain of the everyday requires a recognition that politically consequential ideological action occurs on and between three analytically distinct levels: (1) the canonically defined, or macro level; (2) the intermediate or meso level of competitive political appeals, politically relevant public discourse and cultural criticism; and (3) the everyday or micro level of conceptual use by ordinary people. This differentiation among levels of ideological action and influence helps us to clarify the objects and appropriate methods of ideological analysis. Methods applied in specific cases must facilitate an effective focus on phenomena on one of these levels while still allowing recognition of the complex forms of direct and indirect conceptual influence and connection between the levels.

Making sense of ideological action across macro, meso and micro levels is especially complicated when the main focus is the meso level inhabited by many different types of professional writers and speakers. Such actors draw primarily on non-canonical sources in direct and hence traceable ways. They will also, however, typically draw indirectly on ideas formulated in consciously systematic and conceptually complex written canonical products, which percolate down to the meso level in both readily identifiable and highly mediated, often anonymized and 'popularized' forms. Materials from both levels will directly and indirectly impinge on meso level actors' efforts to convey salient features of 'the political' and to otherwise shape, often intentionally, sometimes unintentionally, everyday citizens' micro level perceptions of and preferences about politics.

The articles in this issue provide good examples of analysis at and between these three levels. Broadly speaking, James Farney, David Laycock, Richard Bates and Howard Brick conduct analyses at the meso level, examining the ideological production, dissemination and conceptual contestation activities of social movement and political party leaders and public intellectuals. These four authors' cases involve actors situated in diverse positions on the meso level of ideological action, some primarily intending specific political changes (Farney and Laycock) and some more interested in making sense of cultural phenomena, or shaping social practices, each of which have unavoidable political dimensions and relevance (Bates and Brick). Perhaps unsurprisingly, the second set of meso level cases were more explicitly connected to canonical works, of either psychological theory, educational theory or national literature. However, even in the first two cases, major actors drew on canonical works of modern American conservative thought while relying rather more heavily on popularized versions and applications of this thought.

The article by Mathew Humphrey, Maiken Umbach and Zeynep Clulow investigates phenomena located primarily at the 'everyday' or micro level of ideological production, modification and use. Their involvement in designing and delivering a 'Massive Open Online Course' (MOOC) allowed them to assemble a remarkable collection of data on 'ordinary' citizens' understandings of basic political concepts. However, in their role as instructors and discussion moderators they were themselves meso level actors, consciously performing mediating roles in their educational, dialogical and ex-post observational interaction with their research subjects. And of course this engagement, and the course design, was informed by their understanding of the theoretical relevance of canonical texts in political theory and historical interpretation. Even in this grassroots research, then, multi-level ideological interaction and relations can be readily identified.

Overview of theoretical contributions and innovations

In this issue's first contribution, Mathew Humphrey, Maiken Umbach and Zeynep Clulow apply morphological analysis to an ongoing discussion amongst non-specialists regarding certain key political concepts. Their source materials for this analysis are the c. 25,000 learner comments from a MOOC on *Ideology and Propaganda in Everyday Life*, convened in conjunction with The British Library in 2015. In examining how learners discuss notions of freedom, justice, and community both with each other, and with the course facilitators, Humphrey, Umbach and Clulow construct a window into lay discourse in political theory.

Using a combination of Freeden's morphological approach to ideology with discourse analysis of learner comments, and an examination of images uploaded by learners that 'represent' each of these concepts to them, Humphrey, Umbach and Clulow sketch a picture of how learners conceptualize and inter-relate these different political concepts. 'Freedom' attracts by far the most learner attention, both discursively and pictorially. Other concepts, such as justice, are frequently assessed in relation to their capacity to protect individual and collective freedoms. Especially in relation to uploaded images, learners portray voluntaristic and somewhat ephemeral forms of community as against more conventionally 'political' forms such as ethnic groups or the nation-state.

James Farney begins our set of four 'meso level' analyses of ideological activity. He shows that it is possible to address questions of the conceptual morphology of comparable ideological developments employing Freeden's analytical framework, while also explaining how the ideas of one ideological movement have influenced social, cultural and political actors in another country. Freeden's approach is familiar to this journal's readers, but its interweaving with policy analysis is perhaps less so. To achieve the casual explanatory objective, Farney uses a combination of two methods developed to study policy processes and adoption, multiple streams analysis and process tracing. Doing so allows him to demonstrate how articulation of specific core features of American social conservatism by meso level players and movement organizations has recently influenced Canadian social conservatism both directly and indirectly.

By applying Freeden's morphological approach in tandem with multiple streams analysis and process tracing, Farney adds a causal dimension to a Freedenite account of meso level cultural constraints and institutional factors shaping the influence of American on Canadian social conservatism. Doing so enables him to argue that while key themes in American social conservatism influenced religious and civil society organizations in Canada directly, there was little direct ideological transfer from social conservative American politicians to their Canadian counterparts. In instances of ideological translation and travel, this distinction between direct and indirect influence assists our appreciation of nuanced conceptual adaptation at the meso level. In instances of indirect influence, contextual dimensions of social organization, culture, religiosity and political institutions powerfully mediate conceptual decontestation, and associated policy applications, without rendering original source ideas from the macro level unrecognizable.

As with Farney's contribution, David Laycock's article attempts to blend, and achieve enhanced analytical leverage from, the morphological approach and another analytical toolkit imported from outside of ideological studies per se. Laycock relies primarily on Freeden's guidance on conceptual morphologies, but also explores the added value of Michael Saward's focus on the 'representative claim'[14] as a constituting dynamic of representative relations inside and outside legislatures and elections. Used in a complementary manner, these two approaches help us to appreciate the logic holding together tax revolts, direct democracy and right-wing populist appeals in the US and Canada in the last few decades of the 20th century.

One key finding in Laycock's analysis is that populism, perhaps more obviously than other ideologies, entails mutual reinforcement of strategic appeals, core concepts and other conceptual foundations. Strategic innovation with either endorsement or use of direct democracy occurs at the meso level of ideological activity to revive popular support for core conservative concepts, whose canonical expression in the work of economists like F. Hayek and M. Friedman is seldom encountered by everyday enthusiasts of the tax revolt. This analysis gives us a better appreciation of how populism has enhanced the political appeal of tax cuts, which has been modern Anglo-American conservative ideology's policy cornerstone from Thatcher and Reagan through the Reform and Tea parties to Donald Trump.

Howard Brick provides another perspective on the operation of ideology in American public life. He drills below the surface of an apparent, officially celebrated 'consensus' about American ideology and values during the time that the US achieved pre-eminent status as a world power. Probing the 'public intellectual' dimension of meso level ideological activity, he shows that in attempting to understand the foundations of 'Americanness', many humanist scholars during the 1950s reflected on how culturally salient self-understandings of American life were a rapidly moving target. As public intellectuals, their ideologically diverse cultural criticism mediated between their engagement with (and construction of) a macro level canonical American literature and an audience struggling, at the micro level, to make sense of the internal dynamics of American society and its place in the world. At a time of government inquiries into 'Un-American Activities', the ideological orientations and intentions of American humanists' literary and cultural criticism belied the homogenous Americanness that Cold War politicians sought to entrench.

Brick defines his theoretical perspective as a critique of historicist attempts to understand and portray specific ideologies as expressions of the Zeitgeist of an 'age'. Exploring the intellectual origins of the discipline of 'American Studies' as it emerged in the late 1940s, Brick takes issue with the ambition to uncover a holistic spirit or animating myth at the core of particular historical moments – something the writer F. O. Matthiessen called 'myth-symbol' analysis – which Brick sees as constitutive of that discipline, and the broader ideology of 'Americanism'. In making this argument, Brick also offers a broader methodological critique of attempts to map distinctive intellectual debates directly onto singular ideological imperatives, in the spirit of the 'historicism' of Giambattista Vico or Benedetto Croce. Likening his alternative method to Dipesh Chakrabarty's,[15] Brick suggests that histories of political thought ought to highlight the contingency, multiplicity, but also the unexpected synergies between competing intellectual positions, to arrive at a more nuanced, complex and anti-determinist view of how ideologies operate at a particular point in time, and, crucially, always also with an eye on the future.

In his original blend of intellectual history with comparative analysis of embedded political ideology, Richard Bates reveals the dramatically different applications and political implications of psychoanalytic theory by American, British and French child-rearing experts in the post-war era. As he argues, Anglo-American experts applied various forms of psychoanalytic theory to guide parents towards democratic child-rearing practices. Their shared anxiety about the political and social risks of conventional authoritarian approaches was, particularly in the case of Dr. Benjamin Spock, matched with a sense of democratic promise. Spock's activities as a highly influential meso level actor in the American ideological terrain were directly informed by macro level political thinker and educational theorist John Dewey. In effect, Spock read and applied Freudian theory through Dewey's political vision, thus, bringing a blend of canonical theory from two conceptually abstract intellectual realms to widespread micro level understandings and applications of childcare best practices.

Ironically, post-war child-rearing theory resonant of Rousseau had considerably greater traction in the US and Britain than in France. Not just concepts but whole theories of psychological development were also decontested – translated from the macro to the meso level – to support dramatically different political agendas, as psychoanalytic approaches were interwoven in France with conservative Catholic views on women's roles and family policy. Bates shows how widely influential children's development author Françoise Dolto came to shape French childcare by the 1970s. She managed this deft mediation between macro level psychoanalytical theory and meso level applications to childcare guidance even though her decontestation of Freudian theory had social conservative roots in Vichy France and anti-feminist thought. In retrospect, it is striking how such applications of psychoanalytic theory were out of step with most strands of contemporary radical – or even particularly democratic – French social or political theory.

Collectively, then, the focus of the articles in this special issue is on political theory as it operates outside of the realm occupied by professional political theorists. Contributors analyse ideological phenomena on the two interlinking levels: the 'meso-' level of those who seek to popularize (or denounce) political ideas in their roles as public intellectuals, political activists or journalists, for example, and the 'micro-' level of discussions of concepts such as 'freedom' and 'justice' by the lay pubic. Such distinctions are inevitably somewhat artificial – political theorists can also be popularizers, and journalists can write political theory. Nonetheless, the essays in this issue seek to understand and illuminate how political concepts that can seem highly abstract in isolation are given 'flesh' and put to work in practical political contexts.

Notes

1. The range of perspectives across such disciplines has been effectively surveyed and assessed in M. Freeden, L. T. Sargent and M. Stears (Eds.), *The Oxford Handbook of Political Ideologies* (Oxford: Oxford University Press, 2013).
2. See, for example, https://www.washingtonpost.com/news/the-fix/wp/2016/11/09/why-polling-faces-a-moment-of-reckoning-after-the-2016-election/?utm_term=.32d731bba0c6; also http://www.independent.co.uk/voices/2016-politics-brexit-donald-trump-boris-johnson-michael-gove-theresa-may-eu-referendum-review-a7484386.html. Both accessed 6 March 2017.
3. See Q. Skinner 'Meaning and Understanding in the History of Ideas', *History and Theory* 8(1) (1969), pp. 3–53, for a foundational text in this influential School. Also Q. Skinner, *The Foundations of Modern Political Thought* (2 vols., Cambridge: Cambridge University Press, 1978); G.A. Pocock, *The Machiavellian Moment* (Princeton: Princeton University Press, 1975); J. Dunn, *The Political Thought of John Locke* (Cambridge: Cambridge University Press, 1969).
4. There are exceptions to this, of course. One such is W. A. Gamson, *Talking Politics* (Cambridge: Cambridge University Press, 1992). Gamson uses focus group research with 'working people' discussing topical political issues. He finds that his subjects are 'quite capable of conducting informed and well-reasoned discussions' about the topics under consideration.
5. See, for example, S. Feldman, and C. Johnston, 'Understanding the determinants of political ideology: Implications of structural complexity', *Political Psychology*, 35(3) (2014), pp. 337–358; J.T. Jost, B.A. Nosek, and S.D. Gosling, 'Ideology: Its resurgence in social, personality, and political psychology', *Perspectives on Psychological Science*, 3(2) (2008), pp.126–36.
6. D. Kahneman, *Thinking, Fast and Slow* (London: Macmillan, 2011).

8 IDEOLOGIES IN ACTION

7. See, for example, M. Rosen, *On Voluntary Servitude* (Cambridge, MA: Harvard University Press, 1996).
8. Even as Marxism has become somewhat less influential in left-wing party politics in western Europe, the 'false consciousness' thesis persists in popular forms, as in the recent moral panics about 'fake news' and right- (or indeed left-)wing populism.
9. Later thinkers from Gramsci to Foucault refined the analysis of socially and economically embedded ideas, and accorded ideological discourse a greater autonomy from the economic substructure than early Marxists had allowed. And we note that Foucault himself was wary of the term 'ideology', due to what he saw as its epistemological baggage. See P. Rabinow (Ed.), *The Foucault Reader* (New York: Pantheon, 1984), p. 60.
10. This is, broadly, the view of ideology on offer in D. Bell, *The End of Ideology: On the Exhaustion of Political Ideas in the Fifties: With 'The Resumption of History in the New Century'* (Cambridge, MA: Harvard University Press, 2000 [1962]).
11. M. Freeden, *Ideologies and Political Theory* (Oxford: Oxford University Press, 1996). This approach to the study of ideology draws some inspiration from some earlier understandings of the concept, in particular the theories of ideology developed by K. Mannheim, *Ideology and Utopia* (London: Routledge 2013 [1936]) and C. Geertz, 'Ideology as a Cultural System', in D. E. Apter, (Ed.) *Ideology and Discontent* (New York: Free Press of Glencoe, 1964), pp. 47–76.
12. This approach was pioneered by R. Koselleck, *The Practice of Conceptual History* (Stanford: Stanford University Press, 2002); R. Koselleck, *Futures Past: on the Semantics of Historical Time* (New York: Columbia University Press, 2004).
13. Here, we can only indicate a few key readings in these areas. These approaches are discussed in Freeden, Sargeant and Stears, op. cit., Ref. 2. On critical discourse analysis, see N. Fairclough, *Critical Discourse Analysis: The Critical Study of Language* (London: Routledge, 2013); also D. Schiffrin, D. Tannen and H.E. Hamilton, *The Handbook of Discourse Analysis*, 2nd ed. (Chichester: Wiley & Sons, 2015); and on historical discourse analysis, in particular, L. J. Brinton, 'Historical Discourse Analysis' in *ibid.*, pp. 222–243. Also S. Shapin, 'Talking history: Reflections on Discourse Analysis', *Isis* 75(1) (1984), pp. 125–30. For a reflection on Koselleck's contribution, see, for example, J. Zammito, 'Koselleck's Philosophy of Historical Time(s) and the Practice of History', *History and Theory*, 43 (2004), pp.124–135.
14. M. Saward, *The Representative Claim* (Oxford: Oxford University Press, 2010); M. Saward, 'Shape-shifting Representation', *American Political Science Review* 108 (2014), pp. 723–36.
15. D. Chakrabarty, *Provincializing Europe: Postcolonial Thought and Historical Difference* (Princeton, NJ: Princeton University Press, 2000).

The political is personal: an analysis of crowd-sourced political ideas and images from a Massive Open Online Course

Mathew Humphrey, Maiken Umbach and Zeynep Clulow

ABSTRACT

The analysis of ideology at the vernacular level requires access to peer-to-peer political discussions amongst non-specialists. It is in these discursive exchanges that political views are articulated, refined, and revised. Such exchanges are, however, difficult for the researcher to capture. Here we take c.25,000 learner comments (along with several hundred image uploads) from a Massive Open Online Course, co-produced by the University of Nottingham and the British Library, as a source of such peer-to-peer political discussions. From five topics we have selected 'Freedom', 'Justice', and 'Community' for close analysis. The idea of 'freedom' generated by far the most learner discourse, being both positively appraised and highly personalized. 'Justice' was generally seen as something to be delivered by political institutions, although accounts of injustice were frequently personalised. Accounts of 'community' often focused on the trappings of nationhood, but some comments, and many images in particular, highlighted moments of ephemeral and more personal, self-chosen communities. Overall, both comments and images show that, in their interpretation of the conceptual vocabulary of politics, people frequently frame their understanding through personal experience in a very direct manner. It is not only true that the 'personal is political', but also, for many, that the 'political is personal'.

Introduction

So freedom for all is not possible without politics, but nor is complete freedom possible with politics[1]

The quote above is from a text in political thought. It is not however, a conventional work of political theory, but rather a comment from a learner on a 'massive open online course' (MOOC) on *Propaganda and Ideology in Everyday Life*, written in 2015. Analysis of the political views of 'ordinary' citizens, taken as complexes of ideas rather than as 'attitudes' or 'opinions' that can be assessed by survey questions, is relatively rare. This is in part because such ideas are often developed conversationally or argumentatively, in interaction with peers. Such conversations are, however, difficult for the researcher to capture as they will often take place in a private or semi-private sphere, and much of their complexity is lost if reduced to answers to opinion polls and surveys. Our suggestion here is that the many thousand learner comments generated by the 2015 run of this MOOC constitute a good digital proxy for just such a conversation between 'ordinary' people about political matters, providing valuable data for understanding political ideas at an everyday level.

Propaganda and Ideology in Everyday Life was co-produced by the authors and the British Library. The course, which is now delivered annually, is structured around five key themes: freedom, justice, community, place and belonging, and consumption and choice. Twenty-five 'learning steps', each prompted by a short video or reading, explore the propagandistic and ideological significance of each of these ideas across a range of political contexts and historical periods, and each step involves intensive discussions amongst the participants. The first iteration of this course ran in May/June 2015. The following analysis is based on the overall experience of participant interactions, as well as more detailed statistical analysis of the comments posted in the first iteration of 2015, which recruited 12,394 'joiners' from over 20 countries. Of these participants, 3881 were 'active' (completing at least some learning steps) and 1585 were 'social learners', posting comments in the learner discussions, and uploading images of how they personally envisaged each one of our key political concepts. These social learners generated 24,871 comments, and contributed over 1,000 images in total.[2] The discussions are moderated, but less than 1% of comments were deleted (due to use of offensive language). Participants responded to the learning materials for that week, to comments from the educators and, in the vast majority of cases, to the comments by other participants. Their images were uploaded to a Flickr site developed specifically for that purpose.

These comments constitute no 'typical' sample of public opinion: they are not statistically representative of the wider population of the United Kingdom, nor any other country or population group. The participants in our MOOC are also self-selecting, motivated to join by an interest in political ideas and ideologies. But they were almost all non-specialists, that is people with a personal interest in politics; as far as we can ascertain from the learner profiles, there were very few academics, practising politicians, or professional journalists on the course.[3] The comments emerged in and through a situation that is not unlike the situation in which most non-specialists articulate political ideas in everyday life: in conversation with others, or in response to 'expert' views they encounter through the media. As educators, we shaped the content of the course, and to some extent we 'got back' reflections on the material that we chose to expose learners to in the first place. However, while we were speaking to learners as academic educators rather than journalists or politicians, the motivation for participants to tack towards the views of the educators was minimal: as one participant wrote, unlike regular students, participants in the MOOC have no incentives to tell instructors what they think we want to hear. There is no assessment on this course, and the vast majority of participants' comments or images were made as part of peer-to-peer interaction amongst learners themselves. What makes them particularly interesting, and different from one-off comments made on other social media, is the sustained nature of the conversation through which they were generated: not as a singular expression of a view or preference, but as part of a discursive working-through of certain ideas, and reflection on how they relate to one's own particular political and cultural experiences, as well as those of others. Because of this, these contributions offer unique insights into how key political ideas such as justice, community, and freedom are expressed and imagined outside the confines of professional politics or professional political thought.

Before we proceed to our comparison, we should briefly outline our methodology. We posed two principal research questions. First, what specific conceptions of freedom, justice, and community were articulated by the participants on the 'Propaganda and Ideology' MOOC? Second, what other political ideas were most closely associated (either positively, negatively, or neutrally) with these conceptions? In answering these questions, we take a 'political idea' to be a distinctive concept that relates to a category or class of potential objects. So, for example, only some types of object, such as power relationships in a particular context, could be described as 'just' or 'unjust'; 'community' requires as its object a particular social group, which can exist in physical or virtual spaces (or both).

The analysis presented in this paper is qualitative and dependent upon the manual reading of comments. However, in order to orientate the study, we fed all participant comments from the 2015 run of the course into Yoshikoder.[4] Through this programme, we searched for word patterns and synonyms indicative of the relevant ideas. This formed the basis of a concordance report which retrieved passages of 40 words (20 on each side) surrounding the word occurrence. These passages were then read manually to identify key themes, issues and other words that were emphasized alongside each idea. These formed the basis of further dictionaries, which were applied back to the concordance results of the initial word searches to identify relevant trends and salience. Thus, we were able to put anecdotal impressions formed during the course to the test, and underpin some of our impressions with a systematic analysis of all comments appearing in the concordance reports.

This is an important process for a data source such as learner comments, as opposed to a more continuous document such as a political speech. For example, concepts are frequently present only because a previous comment is included in a reply, and in this way a single comment (and therefore a particular key word) can occur multiple times in a discussion thread. This can tell the researcher something useful, for example that a particular comment generated a vigorous discussion, but it can also render simple word-counts misleading. The results of this analysis reveal not just particular patterns in how political ideas are held, expressed and contested; they also uncover distinct differences between how particular political ideas are imagined.

Political ideas and non-specialist discourse

In accordance with the discussion in the introduction to this special issue, we propose to study the political ideas expressed by ordinary people as a distinctive field, which is taken as an expression of the political agency of the individual contributors. Of course, all political texts, high-brow and popular alike, form part of the wider discursive field, and no author writes from a position of absolute autonomy, nor wholly controls the meaning of a text. In practice, however, great thinkers are still routinely credited with agency and originality, while it is assumed that 'popular' political thinking follows an essentially collective and derivative dynamic. It is time to test this assumption, and explore the nature of individual voices within everyday political thought.

Such an exploration raises interesting questions about the nature of the sources. Historians trying to uncover the political thinking of ordinary people in the past have often turned to so-called 'ego-documents', such as diaries and personal letters, in order to glean how and why individuals articulate or deploy political ideas.[5] This has generated important new insights about how such political ideas were intertwined with their social aspirations, personal desires and anxieties, and spiritual longings. And yet, historians who have used such ego-documents, such as Stargardt and Duggan,[6] have also been criticized for not reflecting sufficiently on the selection bias that lies in the nature of ego-documents itself.[7] Keeping detailed diaries was a habit most typically found amongst educated middle classes. Particular religious traditions, too, such as Pietism, which place spiritual emphasis on continuous moral introspection, can similarly generate much richer ego-documents than more secular milieus. Another selection bias arises from the fact that people who align themselves with a particular regime or hegemonic ideology tend to reflect on politics more explicitly in their own life writing than those who maintained a sceptical distance, or rejected the official politics of the day. This problem is particularly acute in the study of ego-documents produced by 'perpetrators'.[8]

Ego-documents are, then, worthwhile but limited sources for exploring questions about the relationship between the personal and the political. One thing they rarely capture is that ordinary people, like philosophers, tend to articulate political ideas in conversation and argument with others, rather than in introspective isolation. Diaries are by definition focused on individual experience, and tend to comment on politics only when this directly intrudes into personal life—for example, when soldiers are called up to fight on behalf of their country. Such exceptional circumstances aside, many ego-documents make few explicitly political statements. But this does not mean their authors held no such ideas. Instead of writing them in their diaries, however, they may have articulated these in conversation: with friends and family at the dinner table, in the pub, or when reacting to media prompts. As Charles Taylor has argued in relation to identity:

> We are expected to develop our own opinions, outlook, stances to things, to a considerable degree through solitary reflection. But this is not how things work with important issues, such as the definition of our identity. We define this always in dialogue with, sometimes in struggle against, the identities our significant others want to recognise in us.[9]

We suggest that this is true of individual political beliefs more broadly; they are forged in the heat of dialogue. To grasp the formation of ideas in such conversations, we need sources that are simultaneously personal, and conversational. The learner comments on *Ideology and Propaganda in Everyday Life* possess these conversational characteristics.

The five political ideas at the heart of our course share several important characteristics: all are invoked across a wide range of ideological milieus, and all are nearly always positively appraised. Very few people overtly oppose freedom, justice, belonging to a place or community.[10] Yet despite the generally positive appeal of these concepts, people interpret them in very distinctive ways. This is true for private individuals as much as for formal political movements and theories. A communist vision of, say, freedom or community differs radically from a fascist vision of freedom or community, or a liberal-capitalist one. Even within particular political milieus, these ideas are imagined differently: freedom and justice mean something different to liberals and conservatives operating within the same polity, and sharing the same commitment to basic constitutional principles. Within liberalism, too, we can find different understandings of these ideas, e.g. between neo-liberals, classical liberals, and progressive liberals. In these ways, our five political ideas are structurally similar, in that they are, to use Freeden's term, 'essentially contested'.[11] They therefore provide an interesting starting point for understanding the political ideas held by ordinary people: they are not, on the whole, either/or choices, but questions of nuanced definition and interpretation, which in turn are negotiated in conversations. Moreover, these are also all ideas with strong roots in everyday culture. They relate not only to abstract questions of constitutional arrangements or economic structures, but reach deeply into more quotidian experiences, values, and feelings. Freedom, justice, territory, community, and consumer choices all featured prominently, for example, in recent debates around the British referendum, but they were put to notably varied uses, not just by Leave and Remain campaigners, but also within each of these camps.

For the purposes of this article, we focus on three of these concepts: freedom, justice, and community. In exploring how our participants understand and use these political ideas, we have drawn on the lens of conceptual morphology.[12] For us, the decisive question was not just whether an idea such as freedom matters to people, but how important it is vis-à-vis other ideas, such as cultural inclusivity or social cohesion. Moreover, we are interested in how a particular idea of freedom is shaped by the way it is associated with adjacent concepts, or sub-categories. Defining freedom as a political idea always involves association with other concepts, such as the freedom of movement, or the freedom of trade; other conceptions of the same idea emphasize the absence of particular constraints, such as freedom from state interference, or, as was frequently emphasized in the context of the Brexit campaign, freedom from the culturally alien tutelage of supra-national institutions, such as 'Brussels', or from the perceived power of multi-national interest groups and lobbies. Similarly, justice can be understood as justice for the perceived interests of ordinary fellow citizens, who pay the price for the human costs of globalization, or justice can be demanded on behalf of vulnerable human beings, such as refugees or asylum seekers, who may be fleeing, at least in part, from the consequences of the foreign policy of the countries in which they seek refuge. Community, too, can be inflected differently in comparable ways.

In addition to the question of how ideas are situated in ideological morphologies, however, we particularly wanted to find out how these political ideas are imagined in relation to the lived experience of those who see themselves as separate from, or even opposed to, the formal world of politics. These differences are thrown into sharp relief by the differing patterns that emerged from our evidence specifically regarding the three ideas of freedom, justice, and community. These differences, we shall argue, contain vital clues for understanding the role of individual voices in the formation of political value systems, and for the ways in which some ideas lend themselves much better to an understanding of politics that draws inspiration and authority from a notion of real-life, or 'authentic', experience.[13]

Freedom

The idea of freedom generated intense debate in both our course runs, more so than any other topic. In the 24,871 comments posted 'freedom' was employed 9056 times and 'liberty' (which we take as a synonym) 1043 times. In contrast, 'justice' occurred on 1217 occasions and 'community' 1785.[14] Amongst all these comments, we encountered none in which freedom was not positively appraised. Yet freedom as an idea, and ideal, meant many different things to different participants.

Broadly speaking, participants articulated variations on the conceptual themes of both 'negative' and 'positive' freedom.[15] Many prioritized freedom from constraints. They expressed concerns about the state intruding into their personal sphere, especially through digital media, but also cited manipulations by commercial actors, such as the power of subliminal advertising, as subtly but crucially undermining freedom for modern citizens (see for example. the comment below on smoking). A smaller body of comments identified the 'nanny state', intrusive regulations or high taxation, as undue constraints on a free life (one learner raised the example of legislation against home schooling in Germany). This 'negative' idea of freedom, defined as the abolition of, or overcoming of, external limitations to freedom, dominated discussions.

Some participants, however, explained their idea of freedom in terms more closely aligned with what we could classify as a 'positive' conception, that is, the freedom as possessing the power or resources to act in certain ways. Freedom, to them, was above all about empowering people through such policies as affirmative action.[16] People who articulated this idea of freedom in terms of their personal experience were in the minority, and typically associated positive freedom with political activists of one sort or another. Some participants held that a positive idea of freedom had created the historical foundations of a political order that guaranteed the freedom from constraints they now enjoyed, or sought to protect. Several understood the present political system in many countries as being a result of a historical struggle, in which the quest for freedom was synonymous with the fight for sovereignty against foreign rulers or home-grown despots.[17] Commonly cited examples were movements for national independence from colonial rule, as in India or Malaysia.[18]

We used our concordance results to assess participant comments in terms of whether freedom was taken to be threatened or constrained by internal factors (such as lack of rationality) or external factors (such as state interference).[19] Around twice as many participant comments referred to external barriers to freedom as opposed to internal barriers. In many comments, a correlation was made between lack of freedom and economic inequality. The most frequently cited cause of lack of freedom was the restriction of economic opportunities for those at the lower end of the income distribution scale.[20] The second most cited cause of unfreedom can be grouped under the heading 'society', in other words, the existence of social norms, and potential social sanctions, that militate against free expression of selfhood.[21]

When discussing internal barriers to freedom, participants tended to focus on the question of what it means to make a choice for oneself, what it entails to make a rational, autonomous decision free from extraneous (but not necessarily external) factors. One typical comment was made in reference to smoking:

IDEOLOGIES IN ACTION 15

Have to comment on the analogy with smoking which to my mind left out the power of the tobacco industry that did not give information that allowed the 'smoker' to make a rational decision/fight his addiction for many years. Therefore the power of corporations and advertising subverted the freedom of choice of millions – without retribution – this power structure is also supported by governments happily collecting taxes for a lethal product.

This comment combines both external barriers to freedom (the power of large corporations and government to limit information) and internal barriers (smokers being unable to make a rational choice from their position of ignorance). Ideology itself also featured in comments as a barrier to making a truly free choice, or in constraining the capacity of individuals to think through ideas 'freely'. Participants frequently alluded to social conditioning, which relates to how they conceived of ideology. Ideology was widely seen as being channelled through social and political institutions, such as capitalism, the education system, and the laws and regulations of a society. Significant disagreement remained, however, on the question of whether violence, either by individuals or states, was ever a legitimate means to attaining freedom.

Freedom generated more comments, and more intense discussion, than any other topic, suggesting that freedom was given a very high priority amongst all possible political ideals and aspirations by nearly all of those who participated in discussions. This ranking may in part be due to the fact that freedom was the topic of our first week, when many participants were most eager to introduce themselves and their own political ideas to others. Very few comments suggested that the idea of freedom unduly dominated our political value system, or that higher priorities ought to be accorded to other political ideas or ideals. A discussion about the role of freedom in Islamic societies was the most prominent occasion upon which people asked whether there might be any other goals for the attainment of which ideas of freedom might need to be modified, or even limited in some way, and this remained very much a minority view.

While freedom as a political idea was almost universally supported, its invocations by professional politicians and political parties were not. Many participants pointed to abuses of the concept by political actors and institutions, who they believed had either 'hollowed out' its authentic content, or championed a narrowly self-interested version of freedom.[22] These invocations were contrasted, implicitly and explicitly, with participants' own ideas of freedom. Unlike the instrumental rhetoric of freedom they opposed, participants typically defined their own stance by imagining freedom simultaneously as a political or societal project, *and* as a deeply personal quest and aspiration. Many comments emphasized that the personal striving for freedom was compatible with, and in fact strengthened and reinforced, a commitment to freedom for others. Constraints to personal freedom were frequently seen as applying to whole communities, e.g. on grounds of ethnic discrimination or economic disadvantage; more rarely, gender norms were referenced as constraining the freedom of women. Indeed, equality was the substantive concept most frequently used in concordance with freedom, in comments such as the following:

It is amazing to think that only a century ago women were excluded from much of what was supposedly a liberal and democratic society. Women were fighting for freedom and there can be no freedom without equality.

In opposing such constraints, political aspirations for freedom were frequently imagined as extensions of personal sentiment, and standing up for the freedom of others was grounded in an imagined similarity of personal experiences.

This points us towards an important finding about the nature of political ideas articulated outside the sphere of institutionalized politics. It appears that a political idea gains particularly widespread support, and a high priority status vis-à-vis other ideas, when it is imagined, experienced, and grounded in deeply held individual aspirations and values. This finding is reinforced by the crowd-sourced images from our MOOC. At the end of the first week, we asked all participants to upload an image of what represented freedom to them—an exercise we repeated at the end of each subsequent week on the other core ideological concepts we discussed.

The idea of freedom solicited more images than any other concept. Exact quantification is complicated by two facts. First, because of the constraints of the FutureLearn platform on which our MOOC was hosted, the image uploads had to be hosted on a separate Flickr site; on this, we sourced about 650 images in the first run of the course, which were a combination of personal photographs (or more rarely drawings), and images sourced elsewhere, for example on the internet or in newspapers. In addition to these 650 images, a large number of learners posted written comments that included links to images already on another online platform, usually a website, but some of these contained more than one image, and several learners agreed that the same link or image best represented their personal imagination of the idea in question. Numbers, thus, can only give rough approximations of the nature of the discussion, but it is noteworthy that 'freedom', and what turned out to be a closely associated idea of 'nature', generated 401 individually uploaded images, and a comparable number of additional links, whilst the two themes of community and justice together only generated 223 individually uploaded images, plus a comparable number of links.

In terms of content, it was striking that most images of freedom had an intensely personal quality. Some were photos of participants themselves in a site or situation that embodied their quest for freedom; others, typically downloaded from the internet, showed anonymous individuals enjoying an experience of freedom in similarly personal ways: in nature, on mountains, flying in hang gliders, and so forth. They also included a very significant proportion of images of animals in natural setting, most popular amongst these images of eagles soaring in the sky, and one image of a captive eagle being released back into the wild. Such images express a deeply emotive and personal idea of freedom—but they are not a-political. In fact, many of the scenarios depicted find direct equivalents in what we might classify as propaganda images, or more neutrally put, images that are intentionally and professionally designed and deployed to produce, reinforce, or legitimate particular political behaviours and allegiances, whether by a political party, or for commercial purposes. One participant uploaded an image of the heraldic American eagle as the embodiment of freedom. The many images of wild eagles and other majestic birds uploaded by others may not explicitly reference the political icon, but they subtly echo this heraldic tradition.

Another link to more formal political iconographies relates to the perspectives employed in the freedom images. Many images featured landscapes viewed from a raised standpoint, such as a mountain top or a cliff by the sea, celebrating the gaze into wide-open, often untamed, 'wild' landscapes, as the sphere of true freedom.

Iconographic traditions for such a gaze range from German Romantic paintings from the time of the 'Wars of Liberation' against Napoleon, to the imagery of the American frontier.[23] But while these traditions have undoubtedly influenced the popular imagination of freedom, they are no longer perceived as tied to a particular political moment or location. In other words, the iconography has become so naturalized that people reproduce it in ways that express, to them, an experience that is unmediated, authentic, and devoid of manipulation by specific political actors or interests.

This is not to say that our participants thought of themselves as free. Many used this opportunity to upload an image of the kind of freedom to which they aspired, longed for, and, as their accompanying comments revealed, often felt they were denied in their daily lives. Nature was a favourite locus for such images, many participants argued, because it offers an escape from a world which is mostly unfree, due to political interference, economic pressures, or social norms. Freedom, for most, remained an aspiration—but an aspiration that is immediately accessible through emotion and experience. This, in turn, enables an appropriation even of formal political representations of freedom, such as the Statue of Liberty, into this vernacular pictorial imagination. The statue, which was most frequently depicted in photographs taken from a distance, and often against a golden sunset, speaks, seemingly authentically, to an emotional longing that is not corrupted or diminished by its attachment to a particular historical and ideological moment. The same was true for images of iconic freedom fighters, such as Nelson Mandela, which were the second major type of image uploaded under this heading. Images of Mandela, many participants commented, represent not just a moment in the history of South Africa, but rather, a universal symbol of the human struggle for freedom, as well as an inspirational and authentic leader of this struggle, whose significance transcends any specific political and geographical political context.

Justice

Our MOOC participants' contributions to their online dialogue made very close conceptual connections between justice, equality, and freedom. Justice as equality was construed in various different forms. Most participants focused on financial equality; examples were given about differences in life quality between socio-economic classes and ethnic groups, unequal pay for different types of jobs and also financial barriers to fair trial (e.g. the ability to pay for a solicitor). Justice was contrasted with injustice, and the latter was frequently discussed in quite emotive terms, even if most accepted that interpretations of what is just and unjust could legitimately differ among reasonable people.[24] Comments that linked justice and freedom often focused on the freedom to live without fear of physical coercion, implying that it is the job of the state to apply the law to protect freedom.[25]

Most of the comments about justice were situated within four broad categories: the legal-judicial system, political regimes (including the government and political parties), physical conflict (both its conduct and aftermath), and economic equality. An important element of the discussion around justice referred to the imposition of criminal law. Several participants commented on their experience of providing jury service or, less frequently, acting as witness, observer, or judge in the courtroom, which most appraised positively, as giving them a sense of having a personal stake in upholding the value of justice. Some participants, however, also cited personal experience that demonstrated the presence of injustice in the legal system. For example, some participants shared their insight into cases in which they felt the crime had not been adequately punished. Others had more faith in the ability of legal systems to enforce justice. For example, a former judge provided a detailed insight into the kinds of measures that are taken to ensure a just outcome in the courtroom.

Around a quarter of the comments on justice related to the conduct of physical conflict and enforcement of post-war justice. Several participants weighed the strengths and shortcomings of the Nuremburg trials (a topic for one of the films on the course). The aftermath of military interventions in Iraq and Syria were also frequently mentioned as more recent cases of injustice.[26] Around a quarter of justice discussions referred to particular political regimes to highlight the presence or absence of justice. Out of these, several examples related to the justness of political elites' actions and party-political goals (as expressed in manifestos and speeches) as well as the government's toleration of dissenting opinions and the opportunity for freedom of expression (including speech and protest). A popular theme in the justice discussion was corruption—in the government, judiciary, and workplace and how this is detrimental to the realization of justice. To take one example:

> "Recent protests against governmental corruption in Brazil are based on the idea of an injustice that must be corrected: we pay huge taxes (those of us who are productive citizens) and don't see the money collected in taxes going to Health & Education for the poor. This is an injustice, because we are responsible for those who are not included in the productive system and pay taxes to alleviate their situation or promote their inclusion, not to fund political campaigns meant to perpetuate people in power."

Generally discussions of injustice tended to focus on specific examples (such as the gender pay gap, the allocation of seats under first-past-the-post, or the fate of aboriginal communities in Australia), often related to personal experience, whereas for justice itself, there was a tendency to draw on more abstract categories such as equality and freedom—and sense of a personal stake in justice was much less pronounced than it had been in the discussion of freedom. These findings accord with the work that William Gamson did with focus groups of non-specialist citizens discussing political issues of the day. Here he finds that it is the presence of an injustice frame that can be related to personal experience, which is likely to provide a potential link to political action. Of course, a sense of injustice is set within a broader, if implicit, sense of what justice requires, but it is the sense of injustice that captures people's immediate moral attention.[27]

The images uploaded under the theme of justice were also less personal than those submitted under freedom. The majority reverted to conventional allegories, such as the figure of Justitia, with sword and scales, often associated with court buildings, and a significant proportion of these had a satirical twist, usually as plays on the allegorical blindness of Justice as a blindness to the social and political realities. In others, the scales of justice were distorted by undue influence, such as the power of big business versus ordinary people. A second popular category of images showed protest relating of particular causes that exposed alleged injustices, from Amnesty International to anti-racists or anti-slavery rallies. Some participants uploaded allegorical drawings, such as chained hands breaking free; others showed victims of injustice, such as the abused bodies of slaves. A large number of these images also featured words: they were photos of writing, on posters, graffiti, or citations from famous speeches.

In the comments as well as in the pictures, the majority defined justice in terms of the consequences of its absence: it is visible only where it is denied, and the act of invoking it is to beseech the state, or the international community, to intercede in a particular political or social scenario in order to restore justice. Justice, in other words, was not pictured as a personal aspiration. The state, or some other authority structure—even the football referee was mentioned here—needs to provide justice, and we can demand it from others. But justice was not something that participants tended to embrace as a personal aspiration in and of itself.

Community

National identity was the dominant theme in participants' comments about community, and accounts for over a third of all comments on this idea.[28] But while the idea of community was almost universally positively appraised, the idea of the national community was seen by some as a dangerous, if pervasive, distortion, or at least a partial and sometimes partisan appropriation, of the underlying longing for community. Most comments on national community explored how it is naturalized in daily life, in core symbols of the nation such as the national language, flag, anthem, citizenship, or engendering a shared sense of belonging and patriotism, which for many participants was sincerely felt. Several also mentioned that these nation-based community feelings are intensified when the nation is involved a military conflict. National sports events (especially football matches) were also frequently mentioned as catalysts for a stronger, if temporary, sense of community.

Ethnic and religious groups comprised the second most dominant theme of discussion of community. Both ethnicity and religion were identified as important pillars of community because of their role in creating a sense of shared culture and belonging among group members. This sense of identity was seen as something that could be in tension with the policies of a state, especially where nations comprise diverse ethnic or linguistic groups.[29] Several participants stated that cultural and religious celebrations play an important role in creating and sustaining communities. There were many references to shared norms, beliefs and ethical standards as the cornerstone of community. Comments in this category underlined the role of the family and schools in keeping the community alive by passing on its defining values. Participants also referred frequently to Benedict Anderson's concept of imagined communities and Michael Billig's *Banal Nationalism* (both the subject of presentations on the MOOC) and singled out the sense of belonging and subjective connection as the defining feature of community.[30]

Comments on imagination and community underlined the importance of intentional community-building, including through urban planning and design, in influencing our sense of belonging. One participant commented on Cadbury's model village:

Thinking about Bournville in Birmingham, it was an ideology of how the Quakers saw how its workers should live. There wasn't any public houses or off-licences in Bournville, they wanted its residents and workers to live in a particular way, this is a form of propaganda. Urban planning is a powerful way of making us choose how to live within a type of community.

Several comments in this category referred to (and often criticized) the influence that national governments possess over communities through national education and the media.[31] Several participants gave examples of these types of influence from their own countries; propaganda in the Soviet Union was also a focal point. Map-making and national borders also frequently featured as important influences over one's self-identification with a community. Only around 6% of comments on community directly described specific sites or places that are inhabited or 'owned' by a community. However, several comments described a nation's boundaries as a sensitive and important dimension of community. Moreover, the protection of the national boundaries was emphasized by some as a precondition for the survival of post-colonial communities. A small number of participants referred to their experiences of living in cosmopolitan cities to draw attention to changes and challenges to traditional homogenous concepts of community. Some participants also shared their experiences of living in different countries and the effect of this on their sense of community.

Community, then, was widely acknowledged as an important political idea that shapes our sense of self and the way we relate to others. Yet unlike freedom, and more like justice, it was seen less as a personal aspiration than as a phenomenon inextricably linked with state power, which in turn could be either positively or negatively appraised, or both (i.e. depending on the nature of the government in question, and thus of changeable political value and legitimacy).

The participants' images crowd-sourced under this theme, however, reveal a contrasting conception of community. Official symbols of nationalism—such as flags, parliament buildings, national monuments, or even iconic national figures—appeared only very rarely. Nationalism, at least in its official visual manifestations, seemed far removed from the participants' personal visions of community. While many acknowledged their familiarity with distinctive national iconographies (e.g. in the way particular places or historical moments were represented on picture postcards, in school textbooks or in children's fairy tales), few participants were ready to embrace such representations as embodying 'their' own, personal imagination of community. Similarly, while many spoke about their experience of community on the local level, these featured rarely in uploaded images. A few participants shared images or maps of cities or neighbourhoods they considered home. Some also shared images of the particular streets they had grown up in, but these were always associated with very particular stories, for example, if the neighbourhood in question had rallied around a particular cause, or against a particular threat.

Without such specific narratives attached to them, there seemed relatively little appetite for an emotional embrace of places that could be 'pictured'. What we did see was a proliferation of images depicting what we might call experiential, and ephemeral, communities. For many participants, the idea of community was best signified by photos of gatherings of people, usually outdoors, who had come together for a particular purpose, sometimes in market places, but more often in the context of leisure and celebration: the open-air rock festival, the national bikers' get-together, a new age campsite. This adds an interesting dimension to the way in which the notion of community operates as a political idea in everyday life. It seems to fall broadly into two categories: on the one hand, the experience of community as an idea that is produced or shaped by political power, for better or worse; on the other hand, a more ephemeral lived experience of community, as people coming together around a shared set of habits or values, which was almost universally positively appraised.

It is tempting to dismiss this valorization of ephemeral experiences of community as not properly political: it involves no notion of formal citizenship, and no participation in the exercise of power. And yet, it is important to take seriously such deeply held beliefs in alternative forms of community. Scholars have recently suggested that in a 'postmodern condition', chosen forms of identity, which are often related to particular sub-cultures of consumption, trump ascribed collective identities as defined by sociologists, marketers, or demographers.'[32] Membership in such communities is defined not by (more or less) immutable characteristics such as income, occupation, or place of residence, but through processes of what Schouten and McAlexander call 'self-authentication' through 'flow' activities. 'Flow' activities provide a sense of 'being in the moment', of engaging in the relevant activity in a way that provides the personalized benefits of it. Such activities offer a feeling of connectivity with an alternative form of imagined community, whose members are bound together by shared practices and experiences, which, in turn, reflect political values: particular forms of social interactions, but also, in many instances, a feeling of connection with nature, place, or with some ideal of right living. Tellingly, many of the rituals associated with such experiences of community draw on other values that participants expressed in other sections of the MOOC, most notably freedom, and the ability, through immersion in natural environments, to discover or re-capture a sense of natural selfhood.

Conclusion: personalising the political?

Part of the value of using sources generated by our Massive Open Online Course rests on its capacity to generate a dialogical conversation about its subject matter, in this case, clusters of political ideas, across an international and diverse group of learners. This online discussion parallels, to some extent at least, the face-to-face discussions in which most non-specialists would typically articulate their political ideas. As a framework for analysis, conceptual morphology directs our attention to two specific aspects of these learner discourses. Firstly, the conceptions of the concepts that learners are articulating. What do they take justice to consist in, for example? What is its scope? Who are the agents or recipients of justice? This is not always immediately obvious from any individual learner comment, but over several thousand iterations, a picture does begin to emerge, such as the tendency to see freedom in highly personalized terms. The second is, with what other political concepts is the concept under analysis, positively, negatively, or neutrally associated?

So, for example, we see the association of justice with both equality and freedom, in roughly equal proportions. On the former element of our analysis, it is often claimed, by feminists and others, that 'the personal is political',[33] while our analysis shows that for many people, it is also true that the political is personal, but only across some quite specific political domains. Freedom is conceived in highly personalistic terms, as something that people want to achieve for themselves across different conceptions of the concept. There is a recognition that collectives can be more or less free, as expressed in some commentaries on anti-colonial struggle, for example. However, in both comments and, especially, images, freedom is portrayed as the release of the individual *from* the constraints of politics and society. Likewise *in*justice is conceived in personalized terms— it is something visited upon identifiable people—oneself or others, and even when visited upon entire groups, certain individuals, such as Nelson Mandela or Martin Luther King Jr., can become emblematic of a broader struggle for justice. Other political concepts, such as justice or community, appear to be conceived in less personalized terms, or at least not so much in terms of individual aspirations, and more in terms of institutional and collective forms of political life. Our findings also suggest that for many participants, the concepts of freedom, justice, and equality sit in a mutually supportive relationship.[34] Economic inequality was seen by most as a major impediment to freedom for those at the bottom of the income distribution, as the poor are denied life-chances that their better-off peers can take for granted. Furthermore, participants were as likely to associate justice with freedom as associate it with equality—justice was taken to be that which guarantees our freedom to make choices for ourselves.

A striking feature of the uploaded images was the fluidity with which they traverse specific countries and cultures. As we have seen, for many learners, the Statue of Liberty is an important icon of freedom; others replicate such official symbols in more mediated, and hence more personalized form: the eagle flying into the sunset is a classic example. The nature of our data does not allow us to offer statistically precise correlations between the learners' respective nationalities and their choices of images, from self-identifying comments accompanying the images. Nonetheless, it seems clear that the use of such images of freedom was by no means confined to American participants: it is, instead, an iconography of near universal appeal. The same can be said of images that conjure up historical memories as embodiments of particular political value: Nelson Mandela and Martin Luther King were frequently chosen as representing a participant's idea of freedom (some used the same images as embodiments of justice), and their popularity did not appear to depend on the geographical base of the participants in question. The same geographical fluidity applies to quotations from famous political speeches, which were often uploaded as images, either just as pieces of typography, or occasionally as graffiti on public walls and buildings—but not necessarily in one's own neighbourhood or country. In part, these images simply document that modern digital media travel very easily around the world: more easily so, in fact, than the written word, although catchy quotations and mottos seem more mobile than longer political texts. This use of such images also demonstrates, however, that the personal political imagination of our participants is much less confined by regional and national boundaries than suggested by the formal political discourse we might see in the news. Interestingly, values that are experienced in the most immediately personal and emotive ways are often associated with images drawn from a global pool of visual representations and memories. It seems that the more chronologically 'distant' a particular image is, the more easily it is appropriated into the political imaginations of individuals living today. That is not to say, of course, that the same image represents exactly the same thing in different countries: but neither does it represent exactly the same thing for two people who live in the same country but may be separated by class, gender, or formal political affiliations. Images appear to have a particular quality that allows an almost effortless re-cycling and re-coding, so they can be inserted into ways of thinking and feeling about the political that are experienced as deeply personal, and intensely of the moment.

Images of community, by contrast, were relatively more place-bound, although few of them represented communities fixed in place. The communities depicted, however, were typically of gatherings or communal events that people had experienced in person, or to which they had an immediate personal connection, say through friends or family. In the written comments, participants rarely made their definition of community explicit; few commented on whether joining a community was a fact of birth or an act of choice. But written comments did focus on the processes through which a belief in and political attachment to the idea of community comes about. This may reflect the fact that the participants in this course brought a pre-existing interest in propaganda and ideology to the discussion, which was, after all, the subject matter of the MOOC. For all that, the manner in which participants understand processes of community creation tells us something of how community is understood more widely. There was much reflection on the social mechanisms through which a sense of community is created: family, school, churches, and other places of religious worship, and the symbols that accompany this process of creation. While expressing some critical distance from these processes, most participants did not believe that the idea of community was a bad thing; many credited it with creating social cohesion and transmitting values of co-operation and mutual trust.

While national communities featured frequently in the discussions, their symbols rarely featured in the images of what community 'meant' to individual leaners. When personalizing an idea, or ideal, of community, participants focused particularly on voluntary and ephemeral communities, many of which are created through a sense of shared interests or commitments. On a personal level, it may mean much more to share a rock festival, a biking tour, or a hobby convention than to be a citizen of a particular country, in terms of the felt sense of community that one experiences. And while in one sense such ephemeral communities may seem a-political, not explicitly organized for political purposes, they may still depend on, and in turn engender or strengthen, other political principles, such as freedom of expression. This is not to tie the flourishing of such communities to liberal political culture—they may also be supported by populist regimes eager to draw on the emotive power of collective experience for purposes of political mobilization.

Our evidence constitutes a snapshot of the political ideas of a self-selecting group of non-specialists; yet it does suggest some interesting avenues for further research. It may be that populations find discourses around justice and equality relatively distant and abstract, even if they also see these values as fundamentally important. Justice is a strongly held value, but not an individual aspiration: it can be rendered politically effective if it is linked, both conceptually and viscerally, to a specific instance of injustice, real or perceived. That is why 'scapegoating' and conspiracy theories play such an important role in populist political discourse: if a sense of acute injustice can be linked to a specific actor or group of actors, the value loses its abstract quality, and motivates political action.[35] If we are right in concluding that the idea of freedom is seen in more intensely personal terms, closely associated with the aspirations of individuals, it may be easier to make this idea resonate politically, without requiring the political status quo to be portrayed as a deceptive illusion. Even those who feel that they live in a relatively free society, and appreciate the political freedom that their state or social environment grants them, are likely to hold a personal ambition to achieve a greater, emotionally more intense or authentic experience of freedom in their personal lives, and thus feel called upon to take action to realize the potential of freedom for themselves. Community, too, has aspirational resonances of this kind, but they are less pronounced than those of the idea of freedom, and more typically tied to specific temporal moments than to life narratives. 'Justice talk' often draws on broad, fairly abstract notions of equality or fairness, with only tentative connections to lived experience. 'Injustice talk', by contrast, is frequently related to personal stories, which do not, however, translate into a conceptual aspiration in the same way that freedom does.

Such findings, in turn, may tell us something about why certain political frames have proved more effective than others in connecting to the ways in which 'ordinary' people understand and imagine political ideas. It is at least arguable that we saw evidence of this in the 2016 UK referendum on EU membership. A campaign based on themes of freedom ('take back control' from distant Eurocrats) and collective injustice (in that the UK pays more in than it gets out, and that money could be used for those in need in the UK) appears to have resonated more strongly than the alternative, which was based almost solely on the economic consequences of leaving.[36] Similar points might be made about the effectiveness of the Trump campaign in the 2016 US presidential elections.[37] These conclusions do not only apply to right-wing populism. Rather, they may suggest why political movements and parties of any ideological complexion that effectively frame their agendas in terms that speak to the nexus between the personal and the political gain more traction with voters than others. This is perhaps the most significant explanatory benefit to emerge from our analysis of the MOOC participants. The deep entanglement of personal sentiment, affect, and identity performance on the one hand, and formal political ideas and ideologies on the other, does of course have a long history. But it is an interface that is only likely to increase in significance in future, as digital platforms such as Facebook and Twitter energize and make visible the juncture between the personal and political dimensions of people's lives and experience in innovative and increasingly prevalent ways. This means that understanding exactly how 'the political is personal' will become ever more central to the analysis of politics in the world we inhabit

Notes

1. Learner comment (LC) 'Propaganda and Ideology in Everyday life', 2015.
2. The MOOC is hosted by the FutureLearn platform. All learners who sign up for courses agree to the following: 'You consent that we and our Partners Institutions may conduct research studies that include anonymised data of your interactions with the Website, including Learner Content.'. FutureLearn, 'Terms and Conditions' https://about.future learn.com/terms/ (accessed 7 March 2017).
3. This is not unproblematic as we do not have systematic information on learner occupations. Learners are asked to introduce themselves in the first session and several, although

not all, discuss their occupation. A selection includes an optometrist, several school teachers, a tourism professional, marketing manager, business consultant, and a lawyer. As with the overall demographic of FutureLearn learners, many of our participants had degree-level qualifications, several of which are in humanities and social sciences. As noted, we are not suggesting the profile of the learner community is representative of any broader population.

4. yoshikoder.sourceforge.net/ (accessed 20 October 2017).

5. M. Fulbrook and U. Rublack, 'In relation: the "social self" and ego-documents', *German History*, 23(3) (2010), pp. 263–72.

6. N. Stargardt, *The German War: A Nation Under Arms, 1939–45* (London: Random House, 2015); C. Duggan, *Fascist Voices: An Intimate History of Mussolini's Italy* (Oxford: Oxford University Press, 2013).

7. For a critique of Stargardt in this vein, see R. J. Evans, 'Your soft German heart', *London Review of Books*, 38(14) (2014), pp. 25–27.

8. C. R. Browning, *Ordinary Men: Reserve Police Battalion 101 and the Final Solution in Poland* (New York: Harper Collins, 1992). D. J. Goldhagen, *Hitler's Willing Executioners: Ordinary Germans and the Holocaust* (New York: Vintage Books, 1997).

9. C. Taylor, *The Ethics of Authenticity* (Cambridge MA: Harvard University Press, 1991), p. 33.

10. A partial exception is consumption and consumer choice, which can be more controversial: while many view the idea of choice as essentially positive, others have suggested that in practice it is often illusory, obscuring the domination of production and consumption by capitalist relations. Cf. H. Marcuse, *One-Dimensional Man: Studies in the Ideology of Advanced Industrial Society* (Boston: Beacon Press, 1964).

11. M. Freeden, *Ideologies and Political Theory: A Conceptual Approach* (Oxford: Oxford University Press, 1996), who takes his inspiration from W. B. Gallie, 'Essentially contested concepts', *Proceedings of the Aristotelian Society*, 56 (1955), pp. 167–198.

12. Freeden, *ibid.*

13. For a fuller discussion of authenticity's role in mediating between political concepts and lived experience, see M. Umbach and M. Humphrey, *Authenticity: The Cultural History of a Political Concept* (London: Palgrave, 2018).

14. Each of these concepts had a week on the course devoted to it. Even granted the caveats noted above on word repetition in learner comments, this still makes 'freedom' the most frequently employed political idea by some margin.

15. I. Berlin, *Four Essays on Liberty* (Oxford: Oxford University Press, 1971).

16. 'Equality comes into the realisation of positive freedom when affirmative action is needed to support the disadvantaged' LC, 2015.

17. '[F]reedom is much more important than equality. So first you have to struggle for freedom' LC, 2015.

18. 'During the colonial times we were eager to get freedom from the British rule' LC, 2015.

19. Learners were introduced to the notions of 'positive' and 'negative' liberty through a discussion of the work of Berlin, op. cit., Ref. 15, and others.

20. '[S]omeone raised in poverty might think freedom was just having enough to eat' LC, 2015.

21. For example 'Freedom from government is not absolute freedom provided social conventions still exist' (LC, 2015)—although others highlighted that such norms help to make societies governable.

22. One example comment here: '[T]he suggestion from the DUP [Democratic Unionist Party] to have a "conscience clause" giving Christians the freedom to discriminate against gay people is an example of how politicians use words like "freedom" to suit their own agenda'. Another example: 'most of [our?] politicians now use Freedom to help themselves and their groups instead of other groups or people.' LC, 2015.

23. W. Vaughan, K. Hartley, H. M. Hughes, and P.-K. Schuster, *The Romantic Spirit in German Art 1790–1990* (London: Thames & Hudson, 1994); S. M. Heydt, N. M. Besaw,

and E. I. Hansen, *Art of the American Frontier: From the Buffalo Bill Center of the West* (New Haven: Yale University Press, 2013).

24. To take one example: 'I hate war, I hate injustice and I hate unfairness but who is to say what is just, is my justice somebody else's injustice?' LC, 2015.
25. 'I believe the only way to be free is under the protection of justice'. LC, 2015.
26. '[R]ecent history shows that today, wars are waged that are neither morally justified (Iraq, Syria, Libya) or morally waged (Israel v Palestine)' LC, 2015.
27. See W. A. Gamson, *Talking Politics* (Cambridge: Cambridge University Press, 1992).
28. '[L]ots of people do want to feel connected with their neighbour and part of an identifiable community, and so national soverignty [*sic*] is what they will fight for.' LC, 2015.
29. 'A good European example of how disastrous it can be to hold lots of ethnic minorities together artificially is Yugoslavia, look how that ended.' LC, 2015.
30. B. Anderson, *Imagined Communities: Reflections on the Origin and Spread of Nationalism* (London: Verso, 1983); M. Billig, *Banal Nationalism* (London: Sage, 1995).
31. 'In the civilised world we have to fit into whatever community we inhabit from birth, socialised by our parents, family, other members of the community as well as religions, education systems, laws, and government.' LC, 2015.
32. Schouten and McAlexander illustrate this with the short biography of a Mexican-American surfer: 'His best friends, all surfers, never heard him speak or respond to a word of Spanish. When he married it was to a blonde "surfer chick". Chuck certainly belonged to a subculture, but not the one assigned to him by the U.S. census; he belonged to a subculture of consumption.' J. W. Schouten and J. H. McAlexander, 'Subcultures of consumption: An ethnography of the new bikers', *Journal of Consumer Research* 22(1) (1995), pp. 43–61, at p. 59. On self-authentication, see also Umbach and Humphrey, *op. cit.*, Ref. 13, chapter 5.
33. C. Hanisch, 'The Personal is Political' *Notes from the Second Year: Women's Liberation* (1970) http://www.carolhanisch.org/CHwritings/PIP.html (accessed 20 October 2017).
34. For example, 'I do not believe we can discuss freedom and equality together without discussing justice' LC, 2015. Also 'How can there be freedom and justice without equality?' LC, 2015.
35. The historical connection is teased out by P. Fritzsche, *Rehearsals for Fascism: Populism and Political Mobilization in Weimar Germany* (New York: Oxford University Press, 1990). A discussion of the same nexus in contemporary populism is C. Berlet, 'Taking Tea parties seriously: corporate globalization, populism, and resentment', *Perspectives on Global Technology and Development*, 10(1) (2011), pp. 11–29.
36. On the EU referendum campaign, see T. Shipman, *All Out War: the Full Story of How Brexit Sank Britain's Political Class* (rev. ed.), (London: William Collins, 2017); C. Oliver, *Unleashing Demons: the Inside Story of Brexit* (updated ed.) (London: Hodder & Stoughton, 2017).
37. Tur, Katy, *Unbelievable: My Front-row Seat to the Craziest Campaign in American History* (New York: Harper Collins, 2017).

Disclosure statement

No potential conflict of interest was reported by the authors.

Cross-border influences or parallel developments? A process-tracing approach to the development of social conservatism in Canada and the US

Jim Farney

ABSTRACT
Social conservatism emerged in the 1960s in both Canada and the US as a variety of conservatism that emphasized opposition to feminism, liberalized abortion access, and the expansion of gay rights as critical political issues. Adopting Freeden's framework for ideology analysis, the article examines how social conservatism differed from other varieties of conservatism when it emerged and how it evolved within religious institutions, social movements and political parties in the two countries. It then illustrates that adding a Multiple Streams Analysis approach and process tracing methodology (developed by scholars of public policy) allows for an improved engagement with two 'how' questions important to understanding social conservatism particularly and ideology more generally: how to trace the evolution of an ideology without a clear core of concepts or texts? and, how has Canadian social conservatism been influenced by its American counterpart? Offering short overviews of developments in the two countries, it deploys this framework to argue that American social conservatism directly influenced Canadian social movements and religious communities but not political parties. American social conservatism can, though, be shown to have an important indirect influence on Canadian politicians.

Introduction

Considerations of ideological change and ideational transfer often use the tools of intellectual history and political philosophy. Such approaches highlight the power of the ideas being transmitted and can capture the interaction between those ideas and political actors. In Freeden's morphological development of this tradition, considerable flexibility is developed in identifying the family resemblances that tie together advocates of an ideology who clearly belong together yet lack a shared understanding of the core principles of that ideology amenable to philosophical analysis.[1] The ability to define flexibly, yet consistently, the contours of an ideology is particularly critical when examining conservatism, which lacks the clearly defined core concepts of liberalism or socialism and, as a result, resists a 'textbook style' of definition through the listing of core concepts or canonical thinkers.[2]

This morphological approach has two limitations for which this article attempts to develop solutions, using North American social conservatism as a case study and drawing on developments in multiple stream analysis in public policy[3] and process-tracing in political science methodology.[4] The first limitation is that even Freeden's development of intellectual history has difficulty in dealing with movements which – while clearly ideological – articulate a loosely defined set of ideas and lack a clear core of texts or a canon of thinkers that can be used to define its boundaries. The second challenge is how best to approach the two topics of this special issue: ideological change and cross-national influence. The morphological approach is flexible and offers room within it for the study of the development of ideologies. Where it can usefully be extended is in examining the 'how' of influence and change. It is this 'how' aspect, particularly in coping with multiple plausible accounts of how change occurred, that the multiple streams approach and process-tracing methodology can usefully address.

We begin by defining social conservatism and identifying the place of social conservatism within the morphology of the broader conservative family. Social conservatism is a part of conservative ideology that has emphasized particular parts of broader conservative ideology in distinctive ways, often drawing on religious – rather than political – thinking and emerging clearly as a reaction to progressive patterns of social change. Such an ideological morphology makes social conservatism difficult to define and even more challenging to identify currents of influence and change within.[5] The article then sets out to explain how adding multiple stream analysis and process-tracing to the morphological approach allows us to deepen our account of social conservatism's emergence and evolution. Finally, this article applies those tools to the related questions of ideological change and cross-border influences by presenting short histories of the evolution of social conservatism in Canada and the US. These histories focus particularly on clear instances of ideological influence across the international boundary.[6]

Defining social conservatism

Social conservatives are a distinctive subset of conservatives in North America, both within political parties and within the broader conservative intellectual and social movement associated with them. Conservatism is understood here as an ideology lacking a singular principled core like socialism and liberalism. Instead, conservative ideology is distinguished by its reactive character and belief in the extra-human origins (either divine or cultural) of appropriate social and political behaviour.[7] Three distinctive articulations of conservatism have been important over the past half-century in Canada and the US: free market conservatism, traditionalism and social conservatism.[8] While able to make common cause with each other and frequently intermixing, the differences between these varieties of conservatism are significant enough to cause tension within the movement. Additionally, the Canadian and American mixture of the three types differed, helping to give the conservatism of each country a distinctive character.

For our purposes, what is important to highlight is that each understanding of what it meant to be conservative interacted differently with the challenge to the established order posed by the social changes that began in the 1960s. Centred around a much greater social acceptance of individual choice and autonomy in intimate relations, the political manifestations of this change included the move feminism made to 'personalize the political', rapidly changing social mores around acceptable sexual practices and family structures, the transformed legal and social status of homosexuality, the liberalization of access to abortion, and the end of orthodox Christianity as the defining public face of religion.[9] As these issues emerged as politically important at about the same time in both countries, examining the conservative response to them provides an excellent pair of case studies for examining the question of cross-national influence as conservatives sought to respond to social change.[10]

The dominant articulation of conservative ideology in North America has been free market conservatism. Building on the work of mid-century economists like F.A. Hayek and Milton Friedman, and able to draw both on populist anti-statism and the support of big business, this articulation of conservatism emphasizes the need to reduce the size and scope of the state and to maximize the ability of individuals and businesses to exercise free choice in the marketplace. They emphasize that freedom and economic productivity can be increased both by reducing state intervention in the market and applying market logic in a wide range of social and political contexts. With the neoliberal turn of the 1980s, free market conservatism has come to dominate conservatism in both countries. Its articulation in the US continues to be more hard-edged than in Canada, but conservatives in both countries have moved towards the economic right over the last 35 years.[11]

For such conservatives, the reactive and extra human core of conservatism are understood in a broadly Hayekian way. While social order is important, the key extra-human source of order is the market and the freedom of individual choice inherent in market exchanges. Understood this way, the key change that conservatives needed to react against was the growth of the post-war welfare state and of the economic regulation associated with it. The social changes identified above could attain peripheral status in the free market ideology if viewed as the products of an interventionist government, in the process making family values or education policy a possible point of commonality with social conservatives. But, if they were viewed as the product of or extension of individual choice, then free market conservatives would find government regulation of the type called for by social conservatives problematic. Usually, this piggy-backing was achieved through the articulation of a commitment to generic family values, but free market conservatives were unlikely to see social issues as important even then. If the restrictions on individual choice were the product of religious authorities or if they restricted economic growth and opportunity, these conservatives were likely to come down on the progressive side of the issues. Far more likely to achieve adjacent status in their ideological morphology were positions on foreign policy (especially anti-communism and free trade), federalism (in both the US and Canada, decentralization was attractive to conservatives), or populist direct democracy. Held by free market conservatives as matters of principle, this ideological morphology was increasingly reinforced, for those involved in partisan politics, by changing public opinion.

The dominance of free market conservatism has been long running in both countries. Its increasing strength has meant the total eclipse of the form of conservatism variously referred to as Toryism, traditionalism or Burkean conservatism. This form of conservatism focuses on the protection of the established order, defends inherited hierarchy and is often supportive of an established – but non-doctrinal – state religion. Particularly in Canada, described by one scholar as having a 'Tory Touch' to its political culture, a residual sense of traditionalist *noblesse oblige* underpinned conservative acquiescence to the growth of the post-war welfare state.[12] As articulated by Canadian intellectuals like George Grant, traditionalist conservatism often combined religious appeals and a desire to maintain the British connection with anti-American nationalism and a deep antipathy to capitalist modernity.[13] Given the more straightforwardly liberal nature of American political culture, it is perhaps not surprising that American traditionalist thinkers such as Russell Kirk[14] found themselves further out of the mainstream, and that American analogues to a Canadian Tory like Robert Stanfield[15] or a British Tory like Viscount Hailsham are very difficult to find.[16]

For traditionalists, a concern with social issues could penetrate much further into the ideology – achieving at least adjacent status – than it could for free market conservatives. It was relatively straightforward for them to express concern with the changing public face of religion or to portray the shifting role of women as a worrisome change in the natural order. Grant, for example, made 1973's *Roe v. Wade* decision on abortion central to his criticism of John Rawls' liberalism in *English-Speaking Justice*.[17] At the same time, traditionalists should be distinguished from social conservatives in a number of ways. While committed to a tradition of civil religion (in Canada, sometimes even something like a state sponsored established religion), they were hesitant to introduce specific religious doctrines into political life. Furthermore, they were hesitant to follow social progressives in making such personal matters as divorce and abortion central political topics. Much better, they seem to have believed, that such matters be left to informal social norms and, where definition was truly required, to civil society organizations such as churches. Given the strongly hierarchical nature of their core understanding of order, this group found itself increasingly challenged to make common cause with other conservatives and rapidly lost influence in the 1970s. In Canada, the traditionalists' stronger influence in the political culture was preserved longer, but was in steep decline by 1970 and had more or less disappeared when the Progressive Conservative Party merged with the Canadian Alliance to create the Conservative Party of Canada in 2003. An important part of this decay was the replacement of Great Britain by the US as the primary external orientation point for Canada's political elite.

Beginning in the late 1960s and early 1970s, North American social conservatives emerged as a distinct subset within the conservative movement as they made opposition to more permissive sexual mores, LGBT rights, access to abortion, declining religiosity and feminism core to their ideological identity. Roughly by 1980, most members of the social conservative movement adopted commitments to free market or anti-communist foreign policy as adjacent conceptual commitments – helping them to make common cause with free market conservatives. Other existing conservatives also took time to recognize social conservatives as 'real' conservatives as a result of tensions between groups of conservatives. While some social conservative thinkers are secular, or proponents of an amorphous civil religion, much of the impetus behind the movement came from religious commitments to particular understandings of Roman Catholicism or Evangelical and Fundamentalist Protestantism. Taken together, this means that core social conservative commitments entail accepting that 'the personal is political' – a mantra usually associated with feminists – and that there ought to be a sizeable political space given for religion.

For both free market and traditionalist conservatives, these were problematic claims even if social conservatives adopted – as adjacent concepts – principles of central concern to other types of conservatives. For free market conservatives, allowing religion into political life and taking political stances on sexual mores and family structures were problematic. Indeed, for thinkers such as F.A. Hayek, resistance to such commitments was crucial to their self-definition as classical liberals rather than conservatives. For more practical politicians committed to what became known as neoliberal agenda, such as Brian Mulroney and Ronald Reagan, social conservatives were to be carefully managed as coalition partners so that their electoral support could be maximized while their policy influence was minimized. For traditionalists, the confrontational way in which many social conservatives approached politics and appealed directly to religious sources of authority was problematic. While these fault lines could be papered over, they have remained more or less a constant presence on the North American right since the 1970s.

This complicated history requires us to make some simplifying assumptions about the character of social conservatism as we turn from definition to the question of evolution and influence. First, influence can reasonably be expected to run from the larger and more vibrant American movement to the Canadian one. Second, such influence will be most visible at moments of transition, such as the emergence of abortion as a political issue in the 1970s and the transition of social conservative attention from abortion to LGBT rights in the late 1990s. Third, influence must be understood not as only as adapting a particular formalized ideological re-interpretation but also as a rather loose adapting of tactics, arguments and terminological definitions. Fourth, influence can run through civil society channels like religious bodies, non-profit organizations or the media, just as strongly as through links between advocacy groups and political parties. Finally, in the absence of clear evidence of transnational influence, the default assumption ought to be that ideological evolution is the result of indigenous processes and pressures.

Approaching ideological evolution and influence

Taking these ideological characteristics and simplifying assumptions as a starting point allows us to focus on the influence of external forces on the evolution of an ideology and, particularly, how can we understand American influences on Canadian social conservatism? Freeden identifies ideologies as 'ideational formations consisting of political concepts'[18] which may have strong unconscious elements and are often not as internally consistent as philosophy would like them to be.[19] This is roughly analogous to what scholars in comparative politics refer to as ideas that are 'abstract; systematic, and co-ordinated; and marked by integrated assertions, theories and goals'.[20] Those working in the institutionalist tradition in political science and political sociology have extensively examined the impact of ideas on policy outcomes, paying particular attention to how ideas interact with institutions and interests.[21] In public policy studies, this focus on the influence of ideas and their genesis has been particularly developed within the 'multiple streams' approach.[22] This approach has its genesis in John Kingdon's classic *Agendas, Alternatives, and Public Policies*.[23] Kingdon examines how and why some ideas become influential amongst policymakers under conditions of ambiguity, competition for attention, imperfect information, actors with limited time and attention, and non-rational decision-making processes.

32   IDEOLOGIES IN ACTION

If we accept that Freeden's political theory approach and the ideational approach of public policy scholars such as Kingdon are engaging with different aspects of the same phenomenon, then the focus of public policy scholars on the empirical tracing of outcomes offers some very useful ways to understand ideological influence and evolution. In particular, we could think of the evolution of social conservatism in each country as three strands that at particular moments, under particular pressures, and aided by particular policy entrepreneurs, are woven together to create windows of openness for ideational change. The multiple streams ought not to be thought of as the working out of mechanistic forces, but rather as processes of persuasion and bargaining in which the content of the ideas being promoted is of significant importance.[24]

Kingdon and much multiple streams analysis focuses on different functional streams operating in government agencies. Adapting this approach to our case studies, we can say that the streams in the development of social conservatism are navigated by people engaged in three environments that usually operate separately: the development of religious ideas within religious institutions, the development of conservatism present in social movements and the development of conservative partisan identity present in political parties. While these obviously overlap to some degree, they typically evolve separately. It is when these streams come together that we see substantial ideological change. Two moments (analogous to Kingdon's 'policy windows') are important in the development of social conservatism. In the late 1960s and early 1970s, social conservatives emerged as a distinct group and began the journey to acceptance by other conservatives (a short one in the United States, a longer one in Canada). This period was dominated by conservative efforts to respond to feminism and liberalized access to abortion. The second occurred in the first half of the 1990s when the issue central to their political activism shifted from abortion to LGBT rights.

Allowing a multiple streams approach to define the contours of the study theoretically gives us significantly improved traction with regard the question of change and influence. Recent work in process tracing methodology, especially on explaining-outcome process tracing is helpful for setting standards for identification of these streams. The goal is a 'minimally sufficient explanation' of each case.[25] A persuasive account of influence and change should – at the very least – be able to minimize the gaps in the narrative chain of each stream. Each link in the process is understood as necessary (though not necessarily sufficient) and can be a conglomeration of systematic (theoretically generalizable) and case-specific necessary factors.[26] Properly done, the explanation should also offer an account of the context within which the process proceeds. Thinking of cross-national ideological influence in a way inspired by Kingdon implies that similarities in how ideas changed or movements evolved in two countries are not, of itself, evidence of influence. After all, such developments can logically be the result simply of similarities between the two countries or of an independent third source. Instead, influence is demonstrated by identifying one or more definable processes or streams by which actors in one country influence those in another.

Social conservatism in the US

Taking a multiple streams approach to the evolution of social conservatism in the US entails examining the ideology held by actors in religious organizations, the Republican Party and religious institutions. In an article of this length, such connections can only be sketched, with particular attention paid to junctures that created moments of ideological change or created dynamics that were particularly influential in Canada.[27] One of the critical elements of the story of American conservatism is that it was not closely tied to either political party until the late 1970s. In the 1950s and 1960s, ideological conservatives could be found in both the Republicans and the Democrats and, instead of partisan bonds, they were linked together by self-conscious groups of conservative intellectuals and activists operating alongside party organizations.

At the core of this movement were the ideas of the 'fusionist' group of ideological conservatives centred around William F. Buckley and the journal he founded in 1955, the *National Review*. This intellectual core brought together a wide spectrum of free-market conservatives and traditionalists even as it marginalized those parts of the movement, such as the John Birch Society, that were seen as too radical. As Buckley saw it, the core commitments of this movement were to limited government, opposition to social engineering, anti-Communism and opposition to the United Nations, intellectual traditionalism, and to the general desirability of the free market system.[28] In the 1950s and 1960s, many of those involved in this movement saw religion – often Catholicism – as an important resource for conservatives but specifically religious or social issues had not yet become major points of focus or contention.

Linkages between fusionist conservatives and the Republican party dated back to the early 1960s, when a number of people involved with the *National Review* were important in Barry Goldwater's 1964 presidential campaign. This campaign was built around a bluntly conservative set of principles which brought white Southerners, upset by the Kennedy and Johnson administration's recognition of the civil rights of African-Americans, into the Republican coalition for the first time since the Civil War. Goldwater's stunning defeat and the purge of his supporters from party offices in 1965–66 initially seemed a rebuff for the marriage of conservatism and Republicanism. But, in a more flexible form, that alliance returned in 1968 with the Nixon-Agnew ticket. Nixon's appeal to the 'silent majority' of pro-free market and socially conservative Americans troubled by the social revolution of the 1960s had a soft edge compared to those of his more openly socially conservative Vice-Presidential candidate, Spiro Agnew. This combination enabled a Republican outreach to disaffected former Democrats in the South and to ethnic Catholic voters in the north.

These demographic groups, when combined with the Republican's traditional strength amongst mid-Western Protestants, would underpin the party's electoral success for the next 40 years. For all three of these demographic groups, social conservatism was frequently attractive and rarely a hindrance.[29] Social conservatism was an important part of Nixon's appeal to voters in 1968 and 1972 and stood in clear opposition to the counter culture. But it was not the focal point of campaigns more focused on the economy and the war in Vietnam. Neither was there much by way of distinctive socially conservative organizing that could force party leaders to keep social conservative issues front and centre.

Three events of the 1970s created such a movement, creating the electoral impetus that would be fully seized by Ronald Reagan in 1980. The Supreme Court's *Roe v Wade* decision extending abortion access in 1973 was the impetus for the American pro-life movement. The pro-life movement is the longest running element of social conservatism in the US and the element that most attracted Roman Catholics.[30] The proposed Equal Rights Amendment to the Constitution, which received Congressional and

Presidential approval in 1972 but failed to receive ratification from a large enough number of states, was a second. Led by Phyllis Schalfley, a long-time political activist with ties to the Goldwater wing of the Republican Party, opposition to the gender equality amendment mobilized many previously uninvolved women.[31] Last, and most noticeably, was the mobilization of large numbers of evangelical Christians in 1978–80 by the explicitly religious appeals of Religious Right leaders like Jerry Fallwell.[32] Throughout these campaigns, ideological conservative operatives – most notably Richard Vigeurie – worked to build ties between these different groups within the Republican Party.[33]

Thus, by the 1980 election, much of the work of building an ideological space for social conservatism inside the Republican Party had occurred, as party operatives became more conservative, movement conservative operatives became more closely allied to the Republican Party and conservatives operating in both settings understood social conservatives as aligned with them. The prominent place of social conservatism was reinforced by changes occurring within the third stream of American conservatism, religious life. The 1950s and 1960s were something of a zenith for American religiosity in terms of numbers, intellectual prominence and institutional resources.[34] Church attendance was at historical highs, religious institutions had built an extensive network of parachurch organizations such as schools and hospitals, the pre-war Protestant ascendancy had expanded to include Jews and Catholics, and religious leaders were attaining media prominence.

This post-war coalescing of religious sentiment had begun to unravel by the mid-1960s. The post-1964 civil rights movement, the changes Vatican II introduced for Catholics, the beginning of re-engagement in public life by Evangelicals, and a turn away from religious observance at both mass and elite levels all rendered American religious life complicated and uncertain. At the same time, the sexual revolution and a resurgent women's movement put questions around sexual mores, abortion and gender roles into the public sphere. Very broadly speaking, religious groups took two responses to this complicated combination of events. These responses often divided denominations down the middle and created opportunities for believers of different religious traditions who shared common responses to social change to form ties with each other across denominational or religious divides.

One response, concentrated amongst mainline Protestants but also important to liberal Roman Catholics and Reformed Jews, was to see in social liberalization an important next step in the working out of their religious principles. The other response, which dominated the Evangelical community and was visible amongst conservative Roman Catholics and some Jews, was to see in such changes a fundamental challenge to American values that justified religious actors' political re-engagement and created a bridge of shared values between these religious actors over their past theological differences.[35] Over time, many conservative believers discovered more affinities to con-servatives of other faith traditions than to liberals within their own. This situation is perhaps best exemplified by *First Things*, an intellectual journal founded in 1990 by Lutheran minister John Neuhaus (who would shortly convert to Roman Catholicism) with an important group of Jewish contributors.[36]

Reagan's campaigns and administration represented the coming together of these multiple streams into a politically powerful enterprise committed to free markets, militantly anti-communist foreign policy, and some substantial degree of social conservatism. For Reagan, social conservatism was the least important of the three commitments. He gave social conservatives significant rhetorical recognition and did move to restrict abortion access supported through US foreign-aid funding, did not reopen the Equal Rights Amendment, and was slow to respond to the AIDS crisis. But social conservatives generally found that his administration was unwilling to make the policy moves his rhetoric had suggested – most notably by not moving directly against *Roe v Wade*. If social conservatives did not receive what they wanted from Reagan, his success ending the Cold War and cutting taxes meant he sustained his popularity with conservatives until well after he left office in 1988.

The presidency of his more moderate successor, George H.W. Bush, was a moment when conservative principles were being reconsidered. The end of the Cold War made anti-communism a far less important shared concept than it had been, and created contention between isolationist paleo-cons and interventionist neo-cons for control of the foreign policy agenda. Bush's more moderate economic policies mirrored a general reconsideration of whether a full-scale assault on the state's economic role was worthwhile (to which Congressional Republicans strongly agreed in 1994). Mixed in with these conservative reconsiderations was a great deal of right populist energy that underpinned Ross Perot's 1992 and 1996 presidential campaigns and Pat Buchanan's campaigns in 1996 and 2000.

Whether conservatives ought to continue emphasizing social issues was not prominently reconsidered during this period. But social conservatism's critical policy issues (its periphery, in Freeden's terms) were undergoing an important shift. By the late 1980s, Supreme Court decisions and a stalemate in the abortion debate had the effect of shifting contention over abortion to the state level. The pro-life movement continued to be important and prominent, but it had more or less fully developed its positions and allies by the late 1980s. The Equal Rights Amendment campaign had lapsed in 1982 and, while issues such as the place of women in the workforce could still generate controversy, by this time no movement seeking widespread influence could make opposition to women's equality a central political position. Organizationally, the religious right was going through a generation change as blunt televangelists like Jerry Falwell and the Moral Majority were replaced by more politically sophisticated figures like Ralph Reed, leader of the Christian Coalition.

Social conservatism was prevented from atrophying in the face of this transition by the emergence of LGBTQ rights, especially gay marriage, as the critical social issues in American politics in the mid-1990s. The issue could be fitted into their 'family values' narrative, and public opinion (at least initially) seemed to be on their side. It allowed existing organizations to pivot their appeals without seeming to compromise core values. And opposition to gay rights allowed some key civil society organizations – most notably Focus on the Family – to shift their operations towards political engagement. The reactive and adaptive nature of conservatism – once a socially conservative concern with private life had been acknowledged as one of the ideology's adjacent concepts – allowed for a relatively smooth shift in focus. The political success of this pivot peaked in the 2004 election, when George Bush made opposition to gay marriage and a defence of faith values a key component of his campaign.

In retrospect, however, 2004 also marked the high-water mark of post-1960 American social conservatism. To a degree, this was caused by Americans becoming more secular and more accepting of gay rights (although public opinion on abortion has remained generally stable). At a deeper level, 2004 was the last presidential election where the old fusionist compromise defined American conservatism. The shock of the 2008–09 recession, rising tides of nativism, the Tea Party's militant anti-statism, and significant changes in religious practice are changing the character of American conservatism. In the process, social conservative principles are being pushed from their adjacent status towards the periphery of the prevailing conservative ideology. No one would describe the Tea Party movement of 2008–12 or the Trump Administration as socially progressive. And Sarah Palin, the 2008 vice-presidential nominee, was certainly a social conservative. Yet, the 'traditional family' language within the party is less important than a decade ago, the religious appeals less specifically Christian, and President Trump's attitude to women as far removed from that of a 'gentleman' as from that of a feminist. Social conservative organizations have waned in national level importance and the Republican party's embrace of nativism is deeply problematic for religious groups that are foundational to the constituency of social conservatism, though some religious voters are willing to emphasize one over the other. What does seem clear, however, is that what emerges will depend on policy entrepreneurs bringing together the three streams identified here into a coherent ideological position that appeals to a wide enough cross-section of Americans to offer a viable competitive force in partisan politics.

Social conservatism in Canada

Canadian social conservatism emerged out of the same three streams as its American counterpart (religious belief, social movement organizations, and party politics) with similar timelines and central issues that it was reacting against (abortion in the 1970s and 1980s, gay rights in the 1990s and 2000s). However, the character of the internal evolution of its three streams was different, the broader social and political context less amenable, and bridging across the three streams less effective. Thus, social conservatism took longer to be accepted as a legitimate sub-variant of Canadian conservatism, did not come as close to the centre of the ideology, and has been pushed to the periphery of the ideology more quickly and more definitively. As the weaker of the two movements, we can see a one-way pattern of influence, where the ideas and practices of American social conservatives influenced their Canadian counter parts but not vice versa in any significant way.

Two important differences between Canada and the US provide much of the context for the differing dynamic between the two countries. First, English Canadians are less religiously observant than Americans and even within that context, the potential support for social conservatism is far more fragmented.[37] English Canada's religious landscape included proportionately more mainstream Protestants and Roman Catholics, and fewer Evangelicals, than in the US. As in the US, Catholics formed the core of the pro-life movement. However, an important early source of support for liberalized laws on abortion was the leadership of the dominant mainstream Protestant Church, the United Church of Canada. Many Catholic pro-lifers (a more prominent part of the movement in Canada than the United States) saw their opposition to abortion fitting into the Church's social justice agenda, pulling them leftward. Many other Catholics had long-standing partisan loyalties to the Liberal Party, giving that party a small social conservative element that has only been fully marginalized within the last 5 years. Even within the Evangelical community, Canada has proportionately more Anabaptists who, while often socially conservative, are deeply suspicious of mixing religion and politics.[38] Recognizing important differences between American and Canadian evangelicals and that the conservative wing of Canadian Catholicism seems smaller than that of its American counterpart are important to understanding Canadian religious life.

It is also important to note that key cross-border influences are visible in the religious stream of Canadian public life. They became stronger as technology made communication easier and as the British influence on Canadian intellectual life waned. Canadian religious leaders attended American seminaries and conferences, American journals and publishing houses were important in the Canadian religious market, electronic evangelists and Christian music largely ignored the national border, and some important organizations – most notably Focus on the Family – opened Canadian offices. Some denominations, most notably the Anglican Church of Canada, are part of global networks that have been deeply divided over same-sex marriage and gay rights. Less clearly than Anglicans, English Canadian Catholics have been divided between those who emphasize social justice and those for whom life issues are the determinate influence in their political orientation. In all these examples, the conservative or orthodox side of the argument has leaned heavily on American examples and resources. These influences were theological – politics was not their central concern – but played an important role in rendering these religious supporters of social conservatism more Americanized over time.[39]

As in the US, these divisions within religious traditions opened up room for co-operation across denominational divides. This made co-operation between Protestants and Roman Catholics, particularly, more possible as time went by. Sometimes, this meant religious organizations working together on issues. Most visible in this regard was co-operation between the Council of Catholic Bishops and the Evangelical Fellowship of Canada. They have consistently intervened on a socially conservative side in debates over gay rights and abortion but have not seen social conservative activism as their major focus; they lobby on a wide range of issues. As organizations whose major role has been articulating complex religious traditions, they have sought to keep some distance between themselves and partisan politics.

More often, such co-operation took place within ostensibly secular social movements that had social conservative features. Two organizations dominated the movement side of Canadian social conservatism. Campaign Life Canada emerged as the dominant national pro-life organization in the late 1970s. Emerging out of contestation between activists who opposed abortion but did not treat the issue as representative of broader cultural decay and those, clearly conservative, who did, Campaign Life's continuing success defined pro-life activism as socially conservative.[40] It often looked to the American pro-life movement for examples and resources. The second persistent organization is R.E.A.L. (Realistic, Equal, Active, for Life) Women, which was founded in 1983 as an explicitly anti-feminist organization, with some important overlaps between its leadership and that of Campaign Life.[41] Both R.E.A.L. women and Campaign Life generated a good part of their appeal by tying a pro-life position on abortion together with an opposition to the extension of same-sex rights.

Until the mid-2000s, Campaign Life and the broader Canadian pro-life movement emphasized traditional gender roles that sought to maintain women in the domestic sphere and emphasized their care-giving role. This has changed recently, as the Canadian pro-life movement has become increasingly open to groups such as Pro-Women Pro-Life which seek to be both feminist and pro-life.[42] Both Campaign Life and R.E.A.L. Women are undoubtedly Canadian in their origins and primary impetus, but they were both open to American ideas and sought contact with their American counterparts. In the early 2000s, the Canadian branch of Focus on the Family became quite active in the movement opposing same-sex rights. Though legally separate from its American parent, the intellectual and financial ties are very close. Over the last few decades, a number of very small, but highly visible, organizations have emerged that take a much more vehement tone and have been very open to American influences.[43]

There are, then, important commonalities in the social movement stream in the two countries, which can be partially attributed to a good deal of American influence on Canadian social conservatives. And, although social conservatives found a less amenable home amongst Canadian religious groups than they did in the US, those parts of the Canadian religious landscape that tilted towards conservatism were influenced by American religious thinking. But in the political realm, influence is difficult to see and commonalities are less apparent.

Indeed – in addition to the less amenable cultural and religious landscape – the second important factor differentiating the movements in the two countries is that, unlike in the US, Canadian conservatism in the 1960s had a reasonably well-defined meaning and obvious, well-disciplined partisan home in the Progressive Conservative party. No alternative movement analogous to that led by the *National Review* sought to shape a fresh ideological movement outside partisan politics. And, for those with ties to partisan politics, Canada's Westminster system created much stronger disciplinary bounds than are seen in the American Congressional system. Rather than contributing to the shaping of a novel political coalition, therefore, the initial task of social conservatives was to find a home in an existing one: the Progressive Conservative Party of Canada. Inside that party, British-infused 'traditionalism' was still an important aspect of Canadian conservatism, and this pushed Canadian conservatives towards keeping issues of private morality and religion out of political life. The UK's Wolfendon report's central distinction between 'sin' and 'crime', for example, was frequently cited by Canadian conservatives (including the party's leader, Robert Stanfield) in the 1968 debates over decriminalizing 'sodomy', allowing no-fault divorce, and the provision of therapeutic abortions in hospitals.[44] For some members, the distinction pushed them in a liberalizing direction on the grounds that the state had no business interfering with personal decisions. Those who opposed these changes did so without appealing to religious ideals, offering instead considerations of personal ethics that they were careful to keep separate from their political principles. This shared commitment to the non-political nature of social issues was maintained throughout the 1980s, when abortion was a major political issue, when the Progressive Conservative party was led by an observant Roman Catholic (Brian Mulroney), contained a feminist caucus, and drew much of its support from religious social conservatives in Western Canada.

This norm held even as the Progressive Conservative party shifted towards neoliberal economic policies and, in a process that culminated in the 1988 Free Trade Agreement with the United States, left the British connection behind. It was tested when the Supreme Court of Canada's 1988 decision in *R v.* Morgentaler struck down Canada's existing abortion law. Though the government did attempt twice to legislate a compromise position, both attempts failed because the party's leadership did not impose party discipline on the vote. Both in parliamentary debate and in their political organizing, however, there was surprisingly little effort to paint the issue as turning on conservative ideology. Instead, it was portrayed by social conservatives and by members of the party's feminist caucus as a personal moral issue on which MPs needed to freely vote their conscience. Substantive organizing on the issue inside the party was almost unheard of, and party activists or MPs did not look directly to American politicians for inspiration on the issue (although some of them were under pressure from American-influenced social movements such as the Campaign Life Coalition).

Rather than a shift within the Progressive Conservative party, what created the opportunity for Canadian social conservatives to become part of mainstream Canadian social conservatism was that party's disintegration in the 1993 election. Blamed for two failed constitutional packages that had sought Quebec's signing of the 1982 Canadian Constitution, the party fractured on regional lines. In Quebec, which had supported Mulroney in 1984 and 1988 because of his constitutional promise, PC support shifted dramatically to the separatist and broadly social democratic *Bloc Quebecois*. In Western Canada, also for reasons to do primarily with regional alienation, PC supporters shifted to the Reform Party of Canada. The Progressive Conservative Party never recovered from this. Decimated in Quebec, the Canadian right was fragmented between the right-populist Reform Party (and its successor party, the Canadian Alliance) and the rump of the Progressive Conservatives until the two parties merged in 2003. The result of this merger, the Conservative Party of Canada, was dominated by eventual Prime Minister Stephen Harper,[45] who had come to prominence in the Reform Party.[46]

The combination of partisan fragmentation and a shift in the dominant social issue from abortion to LGBT rights (especially same sex marriage) allowed social conservatism an unequivocal place within Canadian conservative ideology. That it was these changes in combination can be seen if the initial Reform Party position on abortion is examined. The party's position was that, as a moral issue, abortion should not be decided through the regular political process but, instead, through a referendum – a fairly clear populist reinterpretation of the Progressive Conservative position that the personal is not political. Issues of gay rights, especially same-sex marriage, led social conservatism to emerge as a visible set of commitments amongst Canadian conservatives clearly aligned with the Conservative Party of Canada.

Why this occurred is not entirely clear. To some degree, the tumult on the right made it more difficult for party leaders to enforce party discipline than is usual inside Canadian parties. In part, it may be that same-sex rights mobilized Canadian evangelicals – who were strongly represented in the Reform Party/Canadian Alliance – in ways abortion did not. Certainly, Stockwell Day (leader of the Canadian Alliance from 2000–03) made his religiously based opposition to gay rights an important part of his appeal. And it may have simply been the party reflecting the views of the conservative half of Canadians who – at the time – were generally opposed to changing the definition of marriage at a time when the Liberal Party was beginning to move in a socially progressive direction. Any and all of these explanations fit within the construction of a social conservative morphology and any and all of them would have reinforced existing pressures for change to the definition of Canadian conservatism.

The commitments were strongly held on both sides. Some members of the more populist Reform Party/Canadian Alliance part of the Canadian right began emphasizing their religious commitments and social conservatism. Progressive Conservatives, alternatively, saw such commitments as deeply objectionable and as a major reason for the two parties not reuniting. But by the time the two parties reunited, social conservatives were certainly recognized as important members of the conservative coalition.

A strong Conservative party commitment to social conservatism – by American Republican party standards – did not last very long. In 2006, one of the promises of the newly elected Harper government was to allow a free vote motion on whether Parliament ought to re-examine gay marriage. After their loss on this matter, re-examining same-sex marriage or other gay rights or re-opening the abortion debate were repeatedly and explicitly declared off the table by Prime Minister Harper. Social conservatives had some influence on the creation of an ambassador for religious freedom (himself an Evangelical Christian educator), in the exclusion of abortions from medical services supported through the federal government's maternal health foreign-aid initiative, and were friendly to a criminal justice reform agenda emphasizing punishment of bad people even if it did not address their core concerns. At the provincial level in Prince Edward Island and New Brunswick, social conservatives actively opposed government extension of abortion funding with, it seems, at least the acquiescence of the federal government (health care is primarily provincial jurisdiction in Canada but is significantly federally funded – a particularly important fact for poor provinces like PEI and New Brunswick).

However, there remained a consistent low-level tension between the stronger stance that social conservatives in social movements wanted to see the government take and the leadership of the Harper government. Harper's Conservatives defined their ideology primarily in laissez-faire economic terms. And they understood that a stronger social conservative legislative thrust would cost it power, given the small proportion of Canadians who support such an agenda. As with any party, the relative mix between principle and electoral pragmatism in determining a party's position is difficult to tell. What is clearer is that by 2010 or so, social conservatives in the Conservative Party were openly questioning whether involvement in electoral politics was even worthwhile, as opposed to a retreat back into the personal sphere and civil society. Whether many have done so is hard to assess. Certainly, they were visible in the party's 2016 convention debates about the definition of marriage in the party platform – although social conservatives were soundly defeated by more libertarian conservatives who succeeded in changing the party's official platform to accept LGBTQ marriages. The winner of the 2016 leadership contest, Andrew Scheer, took pains to clarify that although he was, personally, a devout Roman Catholic, in his view the questions of same-sex marriage and abortion had been settled in law and in culture and he would not challenge that settlement as leader.

What seems to be missing within the evolution of the political strand of Canadian social conservatism is visible, direct, American influence analogous to that exercised by British conservative politicians on Canadian conservative politicians in the 1950s and 1960s. This sets social conservatism off from other aspects of Conservative Party ideology and activity: most notably, the acknowledged importance of American models in foreign policy, economics and campaign tactics. Instead, the American, Canadian social movements and religious organizations received American ideas and then transmitted them to politicians. But this is an indirect influence laundered, as it were, through social movements and religious institutions. American religious ideas, social movements, and partisan politicians are not directly linked to socially conservative Canadian politicians.

There were good reasons for Canadian conservative politicians to deny American influences on their thinking – especially on such contentious topics as abortion and LGBTQ rights. So, there is the possibility that these connections existed but were largely kept quiet. But, such an argument from absence should be engaged only very hesitantly. Instead, it seems safer to identify mechanisms by which American influence was felt in the social movements and religious institutions that are also a part of social conservatism and – via this path – affected Canadian politicians indirectly but, ultimately, powerfully. This indirect influence was present, but relatively weak, in the 1970s and 1980s when abortion was the issue that defined social conservatism. It became more important in the 1990s and 2000s when LGBT rights became the central issue and social conservatism became a more visible part of the Canadian right. As the American influence on politicians was channelled through Canadian intermediaries outside of partisan politics – laundered, if you will – it became wrapped up with internal Canadian dynamics and developments which had a clearer influence on the development of social conservatism. These put Canadian social conservatism in a distinctly different place within the Canadian right, gave it a noticeably different character, and set it on a different historical evolution.

Conclusion

Social conservatism is a reaction to the social changes of the 1960s that sought to move an opposition to liberalized abortion access, the extension of gay rights, and secularization towards the ideological centre of North American conservatism. This effort faced resistance from the interpretations of conservatism that defined the core of the ideology in their own ways (free market conservatives and traditionalists) at the time. Partially by convincing existing conservatives and partially by bringing new members into conservative political parties, social movements and religious institutions, social conservatives were able to find a place within overall conservative ideology even if they did not fully redefine it.

Although clearly ideological in character, social conservatism lacks a clear, defining set of texts or institutions. This poses a challenge for its study, if we are restricted to the usual tools with which we understand ideology. This article has shown that Multiple Streams analysis developed by scholars of public policy can be combined with elements of Freeden's morphological analysis of ideological concepts. This combination offers us a theoretical framework within which we can understand the development of ideas within independent streams (understood here as religious institutions, social movements, and political parties). At critical junctures, those streams are brought together through the deliberate choices of key actors or through the workings of exogenous forces. These junctures can create the environment within which dramatic changes or reconsiderations can occur. In the case of social conservatism, the beginnings of debate about abortion in the 1960s and 1970s, and the emergence of gay rights as a contentious issue in the 1990s, represent such critical junctures. Tracing ideological development within each of these streams allows us to gain a picture of the domestic factors shaping the ideology that are not limited simply to partisan politics. We can, thus, carefully assess the influence of different types of actors both in the development of social conservatism and in its location within conservatism more generally.

Thinking of development in terms of streams also gives us traction in assessing the issue of cross-national influence. Rather than seeking some sort of monolithic influence, breaking social conservatism up into its constitutive parts allows us to trace the different paths and institutional/organizational forms through which the larger and more vibrant American movement influenced its Canadian counterpart. Importantly, it seems that the influence was not primarily from the American political sphere to the Canadian. Instead, it was from religious institutions and social movements in the US to their counterparts in Canada. Once a part of the Canadian landscape, these ideas were then adopted by some Canadian politicians, but usually in ways that downplayed their American provenance.

Notes

1. M. Freeden, *Ideologies and Political Theory* (Oxford: Clarendon Press, 1996).
2. For useful examples of such 'textbook' definitions see W. Christian and C. Campbell, *Party Politics and Ideology in Canada* (Toronto: McGraw-Hill Ryerson, 1996); R. Kirk, *The Conservative Mind: From Burke to Santayana* (New York: Regnery, 1953); and A. Heywood, *Political Ideologies: An Introduction* (London: Palgrave Macmillan, 2012).
3. For recent reviews of multiple streams analysis see P. Cairney and M. Jones, 'Kingdon's Multiple Streams Approach: What is the Empirical Impact of this Universal Theory?', *Policy Studies Journal*, 44:1 (2016), pp. 37–58 and A. Kay and P. Baker, 'What Can Causal Process Tracing Offer to Policy Studies? A Review of the Literature', *Policy Studies Journal*, 43:1 (2015), pp. 1–21.
4. For overviews of process-tracing methodology see D. Beach and R. Pederson, *Process-Tracing Methods: Foundations and Guidelines* (Ann Arbor: University of Michigan Press, 2013); J. Checkel, 'Tracing Causal Mechanisms', *International Studies Review*, 8:2, pp. 362–370; B. Peters, *Strategies for Comparative Research in Political Science* (London: Palgrave Macmillan, 2013); J. Mahoney and D. Rueschemeyer (Eds), *Comparative Historical Analysis in the Social Sciences* (Cambridge: Cambridge University Press, 2003).
5. A characteristic, of course, that it shares with conservatism generally. See Freeden, *op. cit.*, Ref. 1, p. 317.
6. The focus is more precisely on patterns of influence between English Canada and the US. Although Quebec had a link between a conservative Roman Catholic church establishment and conservative governing parties stronger than anywhere other than Ireland before the 1960s, the 'Quiet Revolution' of that decade swept this connection between religion and the state away. By the 1980s, social conservatism particularly and religion generally had almost entirely disappeared from the public space – a disappearance that occurred without seemingly much impact on the Anglophone version of social conservatism in Canada. See M. Noll, 'What Happened to Christian Canada', *Church History: Studies in Christianity and Culture*', 75:2 (2006), pp. 245–273.
7. Freeden, *op. cit.*, Ref. 1, p. 384.
8. J. Farney, *Social Conservatives and Party Politics in Canada and the United States* (Toronto: University of Toronto Press, 2012) and J. Farney and D. Rayside, 'Introduction: The Meaning of Conservatism', in J. Farney and D. Rayside (Eds) *Conservatism in Canada* (Toronto: University of Toronto Press, 2013), pp. 3–21.

9. In Canada, this can fairly be described as a process of secularization – a movement away from religious belief and religious practice as younger cohorts enter the population that hollows up previously establishment religious communities. See Noll, *op cit.*, Ref. 6. In the US, secularization does not describe the situation as levels of religious belief have remained very high and rates of practice declined only slightly. What there has been is a qualitative change in the style of that practice that creates political pressures for something akin to a secularized public square, even if Americans continue to hold religious beliefs at very high rates. See R. Putnam and D. Campbell, *American Grace: How Religion Divides and Unites Us* (New York: Simon and Schuster, 2012).

10. This article focuses on North America, but for an overview of analogous British developments see M. Jarvis, *Conservative Governments: Morality and Social Change in Affluent Britain, 1957–64* (Manchester: Manchester University Press, 2005).

11. The literature on this movement is very large, but for a useful recent overview of this change see D. Stedman Jones, *Masters of the Universe: Hayek, Friedman, and the Birth of Neoliberal Politics* (Princeton: Princeton University Press, 2012).

12. G. Horowitz, 'Conservatism, Liberalism, and Socialism in Canada: An Interpretation', *Canadian Journal of Economics and Political Science*, 32:2 (1964), pp. 143–171.

13. Born into a prominent Ontario family, George Grant (1918–1988) was educated at Queen's University in Ontario and Oxford and taught philosophy and religion at a number of Canadian universities. Grant was a prominent and prolific public intellectual. See H. Forbes, *George Grant: An Introduction* (Toronto: University of Toronto Press, 2007) for an overview of his thought. G. Grant, *Lament for a Nation: The Defeat of Canadian Nationalism* (Ottawa: Carleton University Press, 1995) encapsulates his traditionalist and anti-American Canadian nationalism. G. Grant, *English Speaking Justice* (Toronto: Anansi, 1974) is a strong critique of Rawlsian liberalism that portrays abortion as the natural implication of contemporary liberalism.

14. Russell Kirk (1918–1994) was an American author and professor. His most famous book is *Conservative Mind: From Burke to Eliot* (New York: Regnery, 2001). G. Nash's classic *The Conservative Intellectual Movement in America since 1945* (New York: Basic Books, 1996) places Kirk in context of the post-war development of American conservatism.

15. Robert Stanfield was premier of Nova Scotia (1956–1967) and leader of the federal Progressive Conservatives (1967–1976). Usually seen as one of the last prominent Canadian politicians heavily influenced by British traditionalism, his understanding of conservatism was articulated in R. Stanfield, 'Conservative Principles and Philosophy,' in P. Fox and G. White (Eds) *Politics: Canada* (Toronto: McGraw-Hill Ryerson, 1987) pp. 376–381.

16. Quintin Hogg, Baron Hailsham (1907–2001) had a very long career as a British politician and writer, one of the last major proponents of traditional conservatism. See his *The Case for Conservatism* (London: Penguin, 1945).

17. See G. Grant, *English Speaking Justice, op. cit.*, Ref. 13.

18. Freeden, *op cit.*, Ref. 1, p. 48.

19. Freeden, *ibid.*, pp. 33–37.

20. S. Berman, *The Social Democratic Moment* (Cambridge: Harvard University Press, 1998), p. 21.

21. For the comparative politics literature on ideas see classic works by S. Berman, ibid.; P. Hall and R. Taylor, 'Political Science and the Three New Institutionalisms', *Political Studies* 44, (1996), pp. 836–857; B. Peters, *Institutional Theory in Political Science* (London and New York: Pinter, 1999); and M. Blythe, *Great Transformations: Economic Ideas and Institutional Change in the Twentieth Century* (Cambridge: Cambridge University Press, 2002). See also the reviews contained in relevant chapters of R. Rhodes, S. Binder, and B. Rockman (Eds) *The Oxford Handbook of Political Institutions* (Oxford: Oxford University Press, 2006) and O. Florets, T. Falleti, and A. Sheingate, *The Oxford Handbook of Historical Institutionalism* (Oxford: Oxford University Press, 2016).

22. For recent reviews of this very large literature see P. Cairney and M. D. Jones, 'Kingdon's Multiple Streams Approach: What is the Empirical Impact of this Universal Theory,' *Policy Studies Journal*, 44:1, (2016), pp. 37–58; N. Zahariadis 'Ambiguity and Multiple Streams', in P. Sabatier and C. Weible (Ed), *Theories of the Policy Process*, 3rd ed., (Boulder: Westview, 2014), and M. Jones et al. 'A River Runs Through It: A Multiple Streams Meta-Review,' *Policy Studies Journal*, 44(1) (2016), pp. 13–36.

23. J. Kingdon, *Agendas, Alternatives, and Public Policies*, 2nd ed. (New York: Harper Collins, 1995).

24. Kingdon, *ibid.*, p. 159.

25. Beach and Pederson, *op cit.*, Ref. 4, p. 159.

26. Beach and Pederson, *ibid.*, p. 31.

27. G. Nash, *op cit.*, Ref. 14, is the standard history of the conservative intellectual movement in the United States. M. Brennan, *Turning Right in the Sixties: The Conservative Capture of the GOP* (Chapel Hill: University of North Carolina Press, 1995) a very useful overview of events inside the Republican Party. R. Putnam and D. Campbell, *op cit.*, Ref. 9, is an excellent overview of changes in American religion from both a sociological and institutional perspective that pays particular attention to contention over social issues. For the contrast with Canada, see Farney, *Social Conservatives and Party Politics, op. cit.*, Ref. 8, and S. Reimer, *Evangelicals and the Continental Divide: The Conservative Protestant Subculture in Canada and the United States*, (Montreal and Kingston: McGill Queen's University Press, 2003).

28. W. Buckley, 'National Review: Statement of Intentions', in G. Schneider (Ed), *Conservatism in America since 1930: A Reader* (New York: New York University Press, 2003), 195–201. For a fuller examination of fusionist principles see F. Meyer (Ed), *What is Conservatism?* (New York: Holt, Rinehart, and Winston, 1964). For their articulation by a politician see B. Goldwater, *The Conscience of a Conservative* (Sheperdsville: Victor, 1960).

29. For the history of the Republican Party in the electorate, see E. Black and M. Black, *The Rise of the Southern Republicans* (Cambridge: Harvard University Press, 2002).

30. For a history of the pro-life movement see R. Brown, *For a Christian America: A History of the Religious Right*, (Amherst: Prometheus, 2002) and R. Tatalovich, *The Politics of Abortion in the United States and Canada: A Comparative Study* (Armank: ME Sharpe, 1997).

31. D. Critchlow, *Phyllis Schlafly and Grassroots Conservatism: A Woman's Crusade* (Princeton: Princeton University Press, 2005).

32. On Falwell's Moral Majority and other first generation religious right organizations see C. Wilcox, *God's Warrior's: The Christian Right in Contemporary America*, (Boulder: Westview, 1996).

33. Richard Viguerie (1933-) is an American political operative and one of the pioneers of direct mail fundraising. He played a particularly important role in forming the 'New Right' of the late 1970s and early 1980s. See his *The New Right, We're Ready to Lead* (Mannassas: Viguerie Co., 1981).

34. See Putnam and Campbell *American Grace, op cit.*, Ref. 9.

35. Conservative evangelical and fundamentalist Protestants were sufficiently concerned with these changes that they emerged from the self-imposed withdrawal they had entered after the Scopes evolution trial of 1925 to form the core of the religious right.

36. Neuhaus, who was born in Canada but spent almost all his adult life in the United States, is perhaps the only example of noticeable 'Canadian' influence on American social conservatism. See R. Boyagoda, *Richard John Neuhaus: A Life in the Public Square* (New York: Image, 2015).

37. See Pew Research Forum, 'Canada's Changing Religious Landscape,' accessed at http://www.pewforum.org/2013/06/27/canadas-changing-religious-landscape/ October 27 2016.

38. S. Reimer, *Evangelicals and the Continental Divide: The Conservative Protestant Subculture in Canada and the United States* (Montreal and Kingston: McGill-Queen's University Press, 2003).

39. See D. Rayside and C. Wilcox, 'The Difference that a Border Makes: The Political Intersection of Sexuality and Religion in Canada and the United States', in Rayside and Wilcox, (Eds) *Faith, Politics, and Sexual Diversity in Canada and the United States* (Vancouver: UBC Press, 2011), pp. 3–29, and T. Fetner and C. Sanders, 'The Pro-Family Movement in Canada and the United States: Institutional Histories and Barriers to Diffusion', pp. 87–101 in the same volume.

40. M. Cuneo, *Catholics Against the Church: Anti-Abortion Protest in Toronto, 1969–1985* (Toronto: University of Toronto Press, 1989) and Farney, *Social Conservatives and Party Politics, op. cit.*, Ref. 8.

41. On R.E.A.L. Women see B. Foster, 'New Right, Old Canada: An Analysis of the Political Thought and Activities of Selected Contemporary Right-Wing Organizations' PhD. Dissertation, University of British Columbia, 2000.

42. For an evaluation of this discursive shift, see P. Saurette and K. Gordon, *The Changing Voice of the Anti-Abortion Movement: The Rise of 'Pro-Woman' Rhetoric in Canada and the United States* (Toronto: University of Toronto Press, 2016).

43. See J. Malloy, 'The Relationship between the Conservative Party of Canada and Evangelicals and Social Conservatives', in Farney and Rayside, *op cit.*, Ref. 8.

44. See Farney, *Social Conservatives and Party Politics, op. cit.*, Ref. 8, chapter 5.

45. Two useful biographies of Harper are P. Wells, *The Longer I'm Prime Minister: Stephen Harper and Canada, 2006-* (Toronto: Random House Canada, 2013) and J. Ibbitson, *Stephen Harper* (Toronto: McClelland and Steward, 2015). For an attempt to assess the role of religion in Harper's life see L. MacKey, *The Pilgrimage of Stephen Harper* (Toronto: ECW Press, 2005).

46. On Reform Party ideology, see D. Laycock, *The New Right and Democracy in Canada: Understanding Reform and the Canadian Alliance* (Don Mills: Oxford University Press, 2001); T. Harrison, *Of Passionate Intensity: Right Wing Populism and the Reform Party of Canada* (Toronto: University of Toronto Press 1995); P. Manning, *Thinking Big* (Toronto: MandS, 2002). For a PC perspective on the implications for conservative ideology, see H. Segal, *In Defense of Civility: Reflections of a Recovering Politician* (Toronto: Stoddart, 2000). For a history of the reunification between the two parties, see B. Plamondon, *Full Circle: Death and Resurrection in Canadian Conservative Politics* (Toronto: Key Porter, 2006) and B. Carson, *14 Days: Making the Conservative Movement in Canada* (Montreal and Kingston: McGill-Queen's University Press, 2014).

Disclosure statement

No potential conflict of interest was reported by the authors.

Tax revolts, direct democracy and representation: populist politics in the US and Canada

David Laycock

ABSTRACT

This paper examines ideological foundations of the 'tax revolt' theme in American and Canadian conservative politics, through an examination of two of its most notable expressions. One was the use of direct democracy in California in the late 1970s and early 1980s to reduce property taxes. The other was the Reform Party of Canada's blending of appeals for more extensive direct democracy and lower taxes from the late 1980s through 2000. Each of these relied on a critique of 'representational failure' in their respective political orders. The popularity of direct democracy across North America has been aided by the right-populist analogy between a market that enables consumer sovereignty and direct democratic instruments that facilitate end runs around legislatures – the sites of representational failure – to allow unmediated registration of the people's low tax, anti-statist will. Employing analytical methods and theoretical perspectives developed by Michael Freeden and Michael Saward, I identify shared and distinctive conceptual and strategic/rhetorical elements in the two cases, and suggest ways of developing a 'hybrid' approach to the study of populisms.

Introduction

Sharing a continent and primary language with the world's most powerful nation ensures that many influential ideological fashions and even specific conceptual formulations eventually drift northwards to Canada from the US. The American tax revolt began with Proposition 13 in California in 1978, spread across many American states shortly thereafter, continued with Ronald Reagan's leadership and Grover Norquist's 'Tax Pledge', and has entered a new phase with the Presidency of Donald Trump. The tax revolt in Canadian politics has been less consequential, but Canada experienced concerted tax reduction agitation and policy change shortly after Howard Jarvis led American populist conservatism into its golden age.

This paper considers populist appeals for tax reductions on each side of the border. New right conservatives realized, first in the US and then Canada, that making headway against their old high tax, activist state enemy required them to hitch their political wagons to populist themes and strategic discursive appeals that had once primarily been the weapons of the left in each country. In each country, conservative political entrepreneurs challenged a widely unpopular elite political bargain and elevated popular distrust in established political parties and legislatures. And in each country, establishing a link between representational failure[1] and the necessity of tax cuts was crucial to the appeal of direct democracy in the populist campaigns.

Many commentators on populism have noted the importance of critiques of failed representation to populist party and movement success.[2] These analyses have focused on explaining the political institutional, economic and cultural drivers of this populist success. So we know where to look for this kind of discourse, and why. However, these analyses have seldom examined the internal discursive micro-foundations of such populist critiques.

In this paper, I address this shortcoming in the literature by employing analytical tools developed by Michael Freeden[3] and Michael Saward[4] to examine the Proposition 13 campaign and the discourse of the Reform Party of Canada. First, I discuss the tools and their complementarity for analysis of populist appeals. I then connect the dots between tax revolts, direct democracy, representational critique and populist politics in the two cases, analysing the conceptual logic enabling conservative populist ideological coherence. I show how making sense of populist appeals entails considering the inter-related conceptual underpinnings, strategic decisions and performative mechanisms involved in audiences feeling represented by populist politicians. This provides a new perspective on some key features of the right-populist ideological package and appeal, which has been responsible for much of the conservative movement's success since the mid-1970s. My analysis also suggests the added value of a constructivist approach to the nature of political representation for the study of contemporary political ideologies more generally.

Structure and strategy in North American tax reform ideology

Populist political discourses strategically appeal to a particular version of 'the people,' and strategically adopt 'thicker' ideological messages from liberalism, conservatism and socialism. Modern populisms construct and appeal to an elemental conflict between 'the people' and elites, in which the people have democracy and justice on their side.[5] But the normative foundations of this democracy and justice are not distinctively populist. They are imported from some variant[s] of major ideologies, such as new right conservatism, and strategically applied with an eye to shifting public opinion closer to the key goals of that ideology. Populisms may supply innovative political appeals and attractive vehicles of power to 'the people', but populist ideology has no inherent political purpose.

Understanding a populist discourse thus requires appreciation not only of its distinctively populist concepts, but also how these have been tied to a set of more fundamental understandings about the ends of political and social life. Appreciating how such bridges work entails considering how strategic elements are infused into the populist discursive structure, to foster a strong sense of citizen attachment to 'the people's' political vehicle(s).

The Freeden toolkit

Michael Freeden's approach to the study of ideology allows us to identify overlapping logics which weave together prominent policy concerns, specific kinds of public appeals, understandings of social change and underlying normative conceptual foundations within political discourse. Freeden proposes mapping the morphology of any ideology with core, adjacent, and peripheral concepts. Such a mapping reveals the conceptual microfoundations of the ideology in question. Core concepts are typically basic normative commitments (such as equality, liberty, or solidarity) that anchor an ideology over time. In some cases, an ideology's core concepts can be meta-commitments to political action or understanding, such as the conservative orientation to resist or manage social change.[6]

Adjacent concepts are also basic to an ideology, but analytically ought to be less heavily weighted than its core concepts. They often signify second-order normative concepts (such as conceptions of human rights) or general institutional orientations to political practice (such as participatory democracy or group representation) that are instrumental to the achievement of core conceptual objectives. Peripheral concepts represent policy positions or heavily symbolic features of, or past events in, the political system (such as positions on immigration, trade, climate change, constitutional rights, or a country's war experience). These may be at the centre of political debate at any given time, but ought not to distract us from the job of discovering their roots in more structurally basic core and adjacent concepts.

For Freeden, the dynamic character of any ideology results from the essential contestability of most of its ideological conceptual microfoundations. Every ideology 'decontests' each of its key concepts, especially when these are actively debated outside the ideology, and always in relation to other key concepts. The meaning of equality, for example, is given a party-specific meaning via its connection to its decontested concepts of freedom, human rights, democracy, the market, and gender, all influenced by and influencing the party's (evolving) understanding of equality. Competing ideologies contest the meaning and policy implications of key concepts such as equality, liberty or democracy. These remain a matter of fundamental dispute within party systems and across civil society, but loyalists accept their party or movement's efforts to decontest key concepts in political life.

On Freeden's account, what makes any ideology distinctive is its system of mutual influences and relations among ideologically distinctive concepts – within the core, and between core, adjacent and perimeter concepts. Examining these interaction effects in populist ideologies is tricky, however, because populism does not qualify as a 'holistic ideological contender', given its inability to provide independent and therefore 'satisfying answers to the basic political questions.'[7] Any populism is at best a 'thin ideology' that relies on variants of more established and comprehensive ideologies to provide the conceptual foundations for such answers.[8]

One or two core conceptual foundations may be shared by all populisms, such as a view of a constitutive social conflict between 'the people' and 'the elite', and some kind of account of 'representational failure',[9] or 'popular sovereignty denied'.[10] But even a strong commitment to direct democracy is not a core ideological concept for any specific populism. As an adjacent concept in some populisms, direct democracy is an institutional means towards normatively centred ends, anchored in core concepts of freedom and popular sovereignty. So making sense of any populist ideology involves examining how populist political actors combine their populist appeal, case for 'the people', excoriation of selected elites, representational critique and substantial borrowings from a better established, fuller ideology.

Saward's representative claim toolkit

Populisms' reliance on critiques of elite-captured representation and governance suggests that we should look to theorizations of political representation for additional analytical leverage in unpacking populist ideologies. Michael Saward's recent attempt to theoretically re-cast political representation is particularly promising in this regard. Taking a constructivist approach to representation that has broad social theoretical affinities with Freeden's morphological approach to ideology analysis, Saward rejects the idea that representation is an event or achievement to be taken for granted. He presents it as a complex and dynamic process involving leaders' or other actors' audience appeals, and related claims to speak for, sympathize with and advance the interests of these audiences. Beyond this, however, Saward echoes an important theme in past theorization of populism: claims to represent 'the people' are simultaneously efforts to constitute their identities and generate fields of meaning within which they act politically.[11]

Saward argues that elected and non-elective forms of representation (the latter by organized interests, NGOs, social movement leaders and high profile entertainers)[12] both employ what he calls the 'general form of the representative claim'. In each type, '[a] *maker* of representations ("M") puts forth a *subject* ("S") which stand for an *object* ("O") that is related to a *referent* ("R") and is offered to an *audience* ("A").'[13] In effect, Saward presents us with the microfoundational basis of discursive representation, which he sees as 'an ongoing process of making and receiving, accepting and rejecting claims – in, between, and outside of electoral cycles.'[14] His work on 'shape-shifting representation'[15] explores the complex repertoire of representative roles and 'positions' employed by political actors in their efforts to engage the public.

Saward portrays representation as primarily a process of contingent and contested representative claiming, not mostly focused on electoral or institutionalized 'facts'. This helps to guide our exploration of the conceptual foundations of populist ideologies and ideologies more generally. Beyond offering an insightful addition to contemporary theorization of political representation, Saward has also indirectly drawn our attention to something crucial about its relation to political ideologies. This is the fact that in the logic linking core, adjacent and peripheral concepts in any particular ideology, one can identify the tracks of past representative claims, along with efforts at cumulatively powerful strategic positioning by claim-makers in relation to their intended audiences. These strategically deployed representative claims do a good deal to constitute a populist or any other ideology.

A hybrid approach

Exploring characteristic representative claims in populist discourses takes us into the internal structure of their accounts of the antagonism between the people and elites, of representative failure and of their solutions to this failure. This internal structure is composed of specific decontestations of key core, adjacent and peripheral concepts in the populist ideological morphology, many of whose concepts originate in a more complete, major ideology.

Several examples of conceptual decontestations can illustrate how the conversion from representative claim to key ideological concept can work. In the modern conservative core concept of freedom, in which 'freedom is maximized when the state is minimized,' one can easily hear the typical modern North American conservative politician's representative claim: 'On your behalf, I will work to reduce the government's power over you.' Representative claim residues also help to constitute leftist ideologies. In the typical left-wing politician's core conceptualization of equality, which contends that 'political equality is meaningless without social equality,' one can hear the echo of past socialists' representative claims on behalf of the socially disadvantaged. And the representative claim/ideological morphology connection applies for leadership styles and related legitimations of power that span the left-right spectrum. When Donald Trump declared that he entered politics to defend the defenceless, and that '[n]o one knows the system better than me, which is why I alone can fix it,'[16] he repeated the 'trust me as a strong leader to defend you' claim that has legitimized authoritarian rule before and since.

The idea that many notable concepts in ideologies' morphologies act as distillates of past representative claims has been supported by recent research on populism. By electronically coding thousands of politicians' campaign and legislative speeches, Bart Bonikowski and Noam Gidron have demonstrated the importance and ideological range of 'populist claims-making' in American presidential campaign and European Parliamentary discourses. They show that the 'supply side' of left and right-wing populisms is replete with widely varied politicians' claims about the people/elite conflict and specific aspects of representational failure.[17]

Bonikowski and Gidron's analysis of the frames and content of these claims could be re-cast in Sawardian terms. The discourse they discuss typically entails an appeal by a party leader (maker and subject), about saving 'the people' (object) from failed representation (referent), to an audience. Understanding populism as a 'dynamic and contextually driven discursive strategy (rather than a stable ideology),'[18] they provide clear empirical evidence of the strategic dimension of populist discourse, and that claims-making is integral to its overall ideological morphology.

Using Freeden's morphological analysis, we can recognize key adjacent concepts in explicit representative claims about the political mechanisms required to achieve an ideology's central objectives. Understandings of people–elite conflict and 'representational failure', or 'popular sovereignty denied' are key right-populist core and adjacent concepts, alongside elements borrowed from a more comprehensive ideology. Claims about people–elite conflict and representational failure are unavoidably representative claims: populist rhetoric is meant to leverage alternative modes and conduits of representative activity, not to suppress representation per se. Conceptually fleshing out this foundation of a populism's rhetorical appeal and its strategic path to political success provides an analytical portrait of 'the people', its elite antagonists, and the political mechanisms by which populist actors claim the latter can be defeated.

Calling the legitimacy of established systems of representation into question is central to contemporary populisms,[19] so portraying their strategic dimensions is essential. The 'representative claim' approach blends well with Freeden's analytical framework to suggest how these strategic dimensions connect to populisms' substantive normative foundations.

The Proposition 13 and Reform Party campaigns discussed later both promoted direct democracy as a remedy to representational failure. The legitimacy of citizens' initiatives and other instruments of direct democracy derived from their circumvention of a dysfunctional or corrupt regime of representation, where parties and special interests prevented the people from fulfilling their democratic agency and market freedom. Right wing populisms define the former value in terms of the latter, and also fashion this decontestation of popular sovereignty[20] into a powerful and frequent representative claim.

Freeden's recent account of the power dimensions of 'performative speech acts' and rhetoric in discourse helps us to appreciate how strategic populist framing of political issues conceptually 'intensifies' political speech and entails a form of power in discourse.[21] An emotionally delivered, repetitive, and metaphorically rich negative portrait of elites opposed to the people's will can cut through complex policy details to deliver a powerful basic message. As Ben Moffitt has convincingly argued, this frequently involves message delivery through repeated 'performance of crisis' by populist leaders.[22] Donald Trump's 'American carnage' inaugural address comes to mind in this regard.

In such political communication,[23] intense rhetoric can clarify what is at stake, who the bad guys are, on whose side the speaker fights, and the importance of accepting the cure being advocated. In making such claims, representatives shift from the role of 'agent' to that of 'principal', conveying a message or policy preference to a citizen audience rather than receiving such a message. This inversion of the standard depiction of relations between citizens and elected officials in political representation is increasingly common inside and outside of populist political circles.[24] Yet given the success with which right-wing populists have portrayed themselves as simply instruments of the people's will, recognizing that such an inversion invalidates this claim is crucial to making sense of right-populist representation.

How does this relate to morphological conceptual mapping of an ideology? First, political speech teems with claims about promised, failed or challenging representation. An ideological appeal addresses an audience with reference to the specific concerns prioritized by would-be or actual representatives. What is it about this group's situation that the representative is offering to improve? Whatever the answer to this question, a series of representative claims establish crucial connections to distinctively decontested central concepts in the representative's ideological morphology. Blending Saward and Freeden, we can say that a successful representative claim – one largely accepted by the intended audience – conveys a distinctive and compelling decontestation of multiple and mutually defining concepts.

For example, a populist framing of political conflict portrays the audience as 'the people', to be championed against some set of elites. But inveighing against elites, while politically appealing, does not offer a self-sufficient message; any related representative claim or sub-claim necessarily has a more specific ideological content. The claimant promises to do something for a particular audience ('the people'), however vague. As subjects of the representative claims, the people could be portrayed as hard-working taxpayers, and the elites as either corrupt, rent-seeking politicians or the beneficiaries of a bloated government.

Representative claims typical of recent North American populisms often feature content from new right ideologies encompassing both system critique and policy remedies. But we also need to clarify how the pattern of representational claiming delivers political messages to specific audiences in strategically chosen ways. Combining the basic ideological map theorized by Freeden with a mapping of key representative claims, and clarifying their links of mutual dependence, produces a richer account that ties a political ideology's strategic and institutionally specific dimensions to its normatively substantive dimensions. This is especially important in populist discourse, since its strategic dimensions – all involving what the populist leaders hope are plausible representative claims – are vital to its success.

Leaving an account of any specific discourse of representative claiming analytically unattached to its ideological 'home' produces a formalistic and misleading picture of what political actors do or intend. Political actors are not simply representational entrepreneurs, regardless of their 'shape-shifting' proficiency. They engage public life with particular policy objectives and underlying ideological goals; they make representative claims to serve specific political and ideological ends. So just as the substantive ideological map is enriched by analytical extension into the operational realm of political speech, the operational realm of representative claiming becomes more recognizably political – because more distinctly ideological – with explicit reference to the ideological 'backstory' enabled by Freeden's morphological method.

Both Saward's recent 'shape-shifting' extension of his model, and Freeden's recent emphasis on the argumentative 'intensification' of political speech as a form of power in discourse, stress the 'performative' character of political speech and discourse.[25] While representative roles and 'subject positions' are 'resources for representative claim-making',[26] however, we must also be serious about what the claims made in various roles add up to. They are not just about creative role-playing and asymmetrical power relations between representatives and citizens. Performance of multiple representative roles over time is linked and justified by specific political objectives, which always have specific ideological foundations. These foundations may not be transparent in every populist leader's speech, and they may be only elliptically referenced in campaign manifestos. Nonetheless, a thorough analysis of the leaders' and party notables' public presentations, writings, fundraising appeals and social media communications can reveal key features of any ideological morphology.

One case in point is how North American populist politicians have promoted direct democracy as much to attack the legitimacy of other politicians, political parties and modes of representation as to deliver specific policy outcomes.[27] Performance is crucial to populist politicians role-playing repertoires: they must appear to be reliable transmission belts of the people's will, while still carefully manufacturing policy solutions that appear consistent with that will. But while performance in relation to direct democratic remedies to representational failure is meant to discredit prevailing political elites, it is never ideologically innocent, as we see in each of the cases considered later. Populist leaders' portraits of elite representational failure celebrate the will of the people, but the people's will inevitably tracks the major ideological concerns of the leader and his or her prominent backers.

Analysts of populism often stress the role of charismatic leaders in populist movements, yet seldom theorize the complex blending of representative roles by successful populist politicians. Saward's recent work on shape-shifting representation takes important steps along this path, by identifying broad patterns of spatial and temporal differentiation in representational practices, conditioned by cultural or institutional constraints, enabling features and political actor agency. He suggests that 'heads of state, members of parliament, interest group leaders, protest group leaders, and so on' may exhibit particular patterns of shape-shifting representation.[28] However, Saward does not consider how there may be some clear affinity between the shape-shifting form of representative claim-making, a critique of existing regimes of representation, and a package of other key ideological concepts and commitments.[29]

Populist politics often provide us with examples of this kind of 'over-determined' representational/ideological practice. By calling for enhanced popular sovereignty, populisms of the left or right critique the legitimacy of extant representative systems.[30] And populist representative claiming relies on a 'thick' ideology that fashions most of the populist ideological core. As noted earlier, this core gives normative specificity and depth to the populist critique of existing representative structures and organizations, particularly with respect to the characterization of democracy and the centrality of the people–elite conflict within this critique.

Saward's recent work on the shape-shifting representative stresses the procedural rather than the substantive character of democratic elements within representative claiming.[31] However, in the eyes of their supporters, the legitimacy of populist representative claims rests on not just the perceived authenticity of these political figures, or their ability to keep their promises. Their legitimacy also ultimately relies on representative claimers' invocations of key normative concepts like liberty, equality and popular sovereignty. Populist leaders employing different aspects of the hybrid ideologies at their disposal provide us with a revealing example of Saward's 'shape-shifting' representative, using various roles and resources to fashion a range of representative claims and appeals to distinct audiences. This suggests another reason for blending Saward's account of representation with Freeden's theorization of ideology to produce a stronger analytical perspective on populism than either can offer on its own.

To summarize: blending Michael Freeden's constructivist approach to ideology analysis with Michael Saward's constructivist theorization of political representation yields analytical tools well-suited to revealing the complex interaction between the normative, strategic and performative elements in populist ideologies. The constitutive populist discursive conflict between 'the people' and 'the elite[s]' is always articulated, in public discourse, through a critique of existing forms of representation and claims to offer an alternative that the people deserve. Saward's insights into political actors' efforts to present themselves as their audiences' willing instruments give additional leverage to Freeden's morphological toolkit.[32] And we have seen that representative claims today end up eventually as morphological highlights of ideology. So we have good reasons to consider how Saward's insights can enhance application of Freeden's morphological analysis to the study of any ideology.

In the following section, my discussion of Proposition 13 in California and the Reform Party of Canada will indicate how Freeden's and Saward's theories can combine to shed new light on the ideologies in the Proposition 13 and Reform Party cases. In each of the cases, I highlight three broad categories of representative claims: a set of claims by the populist political actor about who the people and their antagonists are; a set of claims about direct democracy as a partial solution to 'representational failure'; and a set of claims about a particular political agent to implement the people's will. I argue that the key components of these representative claims are rooted in core, adjacent and peripheral concepts of specific versions of conservative ideology. The interaction and mutual meaning provision among these concepts provide the representative claims with not just an aggregate coherence but also a form of collective legitimacy, which strengthens whatever legitimacy accrues to such claims from their acceptance by the intended audiences.[33]

Direct democracy and the modern North American tax revolt: Jarvis and Manning

Insisting on the necessity of cutting taxes whenever possible has been 'the organizing principle of Republican politics since the 1970s.'[34] The modern American tax revolt has origins in the 1960s with Barry Goldwater,[35] and earlier roots in Secretary of the Treasury Andrew Mellon's post World War One campaign to roll back income taxes on the wealthy.[36] But as one can see in reflections by Ronald Reagan on why his 1973 California 'Prop 1' tax reform initiative failed,[37] a compelling link between direct democracy, fixing representation and tax cuts was not effectively established until the victory of Proposition 13. Reagan's Proposition 1 campaign had focused public attention on escalating taxes. It identified 'almost every group which derives status, income and power from bigger government' as the enemies of the tax reform movement and hence of 'the people'. But Reagan and his advisors did not yet appreciate the value for conservative forces of harnessing enthusiasm for direct democracy to a tax cutting campaign.

Howard Jarvis and Proposition 13

By the late 1970s, the American political right had followed Reagan's lead[38] in emphasizing tax cuts, shrinking the state and getting government 'off our backs'.[39] Public distrust in the 'political class' had been broadening and deepening for some time, but the right's case had not caught on with a wide public until the victory of Proposition 13.[40]

California was the perfect spot to kick-start the tax revolt. First, property taxes had risen precipitously there during the late 1970s, during a period of unnervingly high inflation, creating a sense of crisis that was ripe for 'performance'.[41] Second, neither party in the state legislature had made property tax reform a priority, so politicians appeared unresponsive perpetrators of an egregious 'representation gap.'[42] Third, Republican Governor Ronald Reagan beat the drums of low taxes and smaller state before and after his failed Proposition 1. Part of the support for this programme came from the real estate and apartment owners' groups in Los Angeles.[43] Intellectual firepower and public legitimacy for Proposition 13 was offered by well-known economists Milton Friedman and Arthur Laffer. Fourth, the state's coffers revealed a surprising, multi-million dollar surplus just when local homeowners found themselves charged two to three times their 1977 property taxes. Fifth, but still important, California had a storied history of direct democracy being used by activist citizens and popular politicians to fight the railroad company 'special interests' that had dominated state politics in the late 19th and early 20th centuries.[44] Direct democracy was thus at the centre of a local 'popular democratic tradition', to which Ernesto Laclau argued a successful populism must appeal.[45]

IDEOLOGIES IN ACTION   55

Finally, California had Howard Jarvis. Jarvis was a mid-70s, successful small businessman, long-time Republican, anti-tax crusader, and perennial candidate for elected office. He was remarkably energetic, and in spite of his retro appearance and simplistic presentation of issues, he charmed the California media and was a surprisingly effective public figure. Single-issue 'revolts' need leaders with an entrepreneurial flair at least as much as grass-roots crusades, and Howard Jarvis fitted the bill.

Jarvis's United Organization of Taxpayers' 1972 and 1976 attempts to place an anti-tax initiative on the state ballot just fell short of collecting enough signatures.[46] In July 1977 a unified anti-tax group led by Howard Jarvis and Paul Gann started another signature collection campaign. Proposition 13 was certified as a state-wide initiative in December 1977. It called for a 1% cap on the property tax of any assessed property value, and required a 2/3 state legislature vote for any tax increase, not just property taxes. It would ensure major reductions to property taxes, as well as across the board caps on other taxes.[47] In short, it was the perfect weapon in a political war that neither legislative party was willing to lead.

From the outset, Jarvis was the highest-profile advocate for the initiative, going to countless meetings, interviewing on dozens of talk-radio and TV shows, and debating with Proposition 13 opponents. With a disarmingly folksy manner, Jarvis presented his efforts as a crusade on behalf of 'the people' against an array of 'special interests'. His crusade was an extended and often repetitive series of representative claims on behalf of the people against a grab-bag of the people's enemies. These enemies included bureaucrats, welfare recipients, public sector union leaders, and the career politicians in both parties who had refused to say no to these special interests. He denied that he stood to gain from his tax revolt leadership, and basked in his rapid media elevation to the status of folk hero. His old-fashioned appearance, avuncular manner and fist-pounding antics combined with his willingness to take on the state's political elite to produce an unusual form of charisma. His post-Proposition 13 popularity and national profile was so great that when he went to Washington DC after the Proposition 13 vote, many prominent Democratic party leaders felt constrained to meet with him, including President Jimmy Carter and two key Congressional Democrats: House of Representatives Leader Tip O'Neill and Senate Majority leader Robert Byrd.[48] Jarvis's status as 'the People's Hero' was sufficiently important that it qualifies as an adjacent concept in the Proposition 13 movement ideology.

Jarvis extended his campaign's appeal by adding some of the state's biggest corporations to his list of the people's enemies. It was not that Jarvis saw an incompatibility between big business and the people's interests. Rather, he cleverly claimed they had opposed Proposition 13 because politicians had blackmailed businesses into opposing Proposition 13 with threats of higher corporate taxes. Corporate interests were a strategically useful addition to the category of 'special interests' in a state whose earlier populist/progressive tradition had featured the major railroad companies as the people's principal antagonist.[49] But corporations were not his main target. As he put it in his 1979 bestseller, 'I'm Mad as Hell,'

> the problem is that property taxes have been used to pay for the special interests that grew up within the government, such as social workers, food-stamp recipients, aid to dependent children programs – all of these people have lobbies of their own. They are the ones who want more services – not the people who pay the bills. The taxpayers have services coming out their ears already. They don't use all of these exotic services.[50]

Jarvis's Proposition 13 campaign emphasized that elected political representatives had utterly failed to convert hardworking, taxpaying ordinary people's desire for lower taxes and smaller government into appropriate policy. Instead, government action fuelled by the people's taxes benefited political elites and undeserving dependents of a bloated state. With Democratic and Republican state legislators both refusing to act on their behalf, the people needed to override an unresponsive legislature by directly legislating their own tax cut. Jarvis characterized the whole state political system as rotten, with corrupt legislators on both sides of the aisle. This accusation of a corrupt party system was both a key part of a representative claim ('I'll fight for you against a corrupt system') and an important pair of adjacent concepts. First, due to their corruption, politicians could not be trusted by citizens, and second, the whole system of representation was failing them. Jarvis contended that because government was incapable of doing 'the people' any good, only the free market could convert the people's will into acceptable results. Direct democracy was the closest political analogue available to the free market's unmediated expression of consumer sovereignty/sovereign will, so it had to be utilized to achieve the people's real will for lower taxes. This high-profile adjacent conceptualization of direct democracy drew on a core concept imported from the right wing of the Republican party with a characteristic populist twist: citizens are best understood as besieged taxpayers, and the people's real enemies – the true elites – are state-dependent special interests, corrupt politicians and rent-seeking bureaucrats.

This message was skilfully conveyed in a wide range of Jarvis's 'United Organization of Taxpayers' pamphlets and direct mail literature, and in his many public speeches and media interviews. In Freeden's terms, adjacent conceptualizations contrasted the direct and genuine expression of taxpayers'/voters' wills in the market and in ballot initiatives with the duplicitous, special-interest corrupted behaviour of elected officials, bureaucrats and their free-loading client groups. Politics was by a definition a realm of blocked, distorted and ultimately failed representation. This framed a powerful adjacent concept in the Proposition 13 ideology: taxpayers needed to use direct democracy to build end runs around a dysfunctional system.

Underlying this immediate political fix, however, the solution that Jarvis often sprinkled in with his anti-tax, anti-politician message echoed the new right's increasingly influential message: radically reduce freedom-destroying taxes and downsize the state's role in economic life. These crucial concepts in a right-wing political economy and agenda turned on another core concept-driven claim. Jarvis insisted that in most policy areas markets were optimal social choice mechanisms, able to replace elected representatives and government choice. As a long-time Cold Warrior, he often contrasted this path to greater liberty with the Communist alternative, towards which high taxes would drag unwitting Americans. Jarvis may have only read excerpts from Hayek's *Road to Serfdom* in *The Reader's Digest*, but he was happy to convey its message.

In the Proposition 13 campaign's ideology, an anti-statist understanding of liberty appropriated from American conservative liberalism provides one key core concept, and another is an abiding faith in markets – 'extra human origin of the social order'[51] par excellence in American conservatism – as optimal social choice mechanisms. Howard Jarvis's folksy communication of these themes closely connected them to key adjacent concepts: the desirability of taxpayer freedom from high taxes, elimination of costly social programmes, and a much smaller state. If markets are optimal social choice mechanisms, it follows that political representation conveys the people's will much less accountably and legitimately than the expression of their own 'consumer sovereignty'.

None of this ideological foundation would matter to a populist campaign if it did not make an effective populist appeal through a series of 'anti-representational' representative claims. The core elemental conflict between the people and specified elites is framed to make elite denial of the people's sovereignty evident. In constructing the subject and audience of the right-populist representative claim, the people are defined as taxpayers, the true agents of the anti-statist liberty anchoring new right ideology. Elites are associated with the overbearing, intrusive state that blocks the people's freedom. An 'anti-politician' political leader acts as the maker and strategic pivot of a representative claim that combines a promise to fight for their interests against the elites, and a mechanism for circumventing state and other elites' suppression of the people's freedom – direct democracy. The populist claim-maker promises his audience a simple way of recovering their hard-won income, and freedom from an intrusive state, by registering market-like preferences in the realm of public policy. Jarvis's innovation in the American populist tradition was his unabashedly simple and repetitive insistence that 'the people' would only be truly represented by reducing government power over business and reversing the redistributive effect of taxation. This signalled a reversal of a century-long American left-populist tradition, which had contended that the people's real will could only be represented, and the corporate elite will's thwarted, through a more redistributive and regulatory state.[52]

It is worthwhile working through the structure of one of Jarvis's frequent representative claims to see how it acted as the vehicle of his ideology's key concepts. As noted earlier, Saward's formula for these claims is '[a] *maker* of representations puts forth a *subject* which stands for an *object* that is related to a *referent* and is offered to an *audience*.' Claim Maker Jarvis presents himself and his Proposition 13 campaigners as the subjects who represent the over-taxed citizens suffering from governance by corrupt legislators. In this formulation, the people are both object and audience in a potent representative claim, while the referent is a special interest-driven pattern of governance. This representative claim encompasses the core concept of a people/elite conflict, defines the elite as special interests, incorporates adjacent concepts of citizens as taxpayers and over-taxed victims of special interest power/corrupt politicians, and promises deliverance from this sorry state of affairs courtesy of another adjacent concept, a charismatic yet trustworthy man of the people.

A more complicated representative claim made by Jarvis's campaign suggested that while he and his campaign would battle on the people's behalf, citizens (the 'object' and the 'audience') must represent themselves in the political marketplace through the citizen's initiative. This is a kind of 'anti-representative' representative claim: voting for Proposition 13 will allow them to avoid the distorting, corrupt mediation of citizen preferences by parties, organized interests, bureaucrats and compromised businessmen. Jarvis presented this as a perversion of true democratic representation that had diminished their freedom by allowing politics to trump markets as social choice mechanisms. We can formally separate the substantive content of the new right normative and institutional core from the strategic appeal and mechanisms featured in the campaign's representative claims, However, in practice they are co-dependent elements of a dense rhetorical, strategic and conceptual populist package, which we can analytically prise apart more easily with help from both Freeden and Saward.

Proposition 13 won with just over 65% of the votes cast in July 1978. Jarvis had successfully made representational claims to the people about the nature of the political game, its major combatants, and the direct democratic means of their salvation. Voters responded positively across ethnic, income, regional and educational boundaries. In practice, however, the benefits accrued primarily to middle- and upper-income Californians, and excluded many non-white, non-middle-class, non-home-owning taxpayers.[53]

Several years following the Proposition 13 vote, California's public services began a long decline. The once nation-leading public school system dropped to the bottom half of state system rankings. Ironically, restricting local governments' revenue by slashing property taxes meant that the state government had more control over local services. Voters thus used Proposition 13 to transfer more power to exactly the state legislature that Jarvis had excoriated as being out of touch with and antagonistic to taxpayers' interests.[54] Californians passed several later tax-limiting initiatives, including Paul Gann's 'Son of 13' Proposition 9 in 1979, Proposition 62[55] in 1986 and Proposition 218 in 1996.[56]

After Proposition 13, government bashing and promises of major tax cuts took centre stage in Ronald Reagan's ascent to leadership and re-direction of the Republican party beyond California.[57] In 1978 Reagan suggested that Jarvis had won an important battle in a longer war.[58] Jarvis's personal papers reveal his delight in being an invited guest at Reagan's first inauguration, to see Reagan respond in 1981 to pressure from Jarvis's and other tax reform organizations with large income tax cuts, and to have photo ops with Reagan in the Oval Office.

The success of Proposition 13 triggered a rapid uptake of populist rhetorical style and strategy among American conservatives. As Howard Phillips, National Director of the 'Conservative Caucus'[59] put it in 1984, 'the real battle in America today is not between Republicans and Democrats, but one which has a greedy establishment elite using the tax process to prey on the working people of our nation.'[60] This passage encapsulates how conservatives creatively built a multi-layered, powerful populist representative claim on behalf of the people and against elites. Doing so would have seemed bizarre to earlier American conservatives, for whom attacks on 'the elite' in the name of 'the working people' would have seemed the stuff of left-wing delusion. With Trump's success in retaining his working-class constituency, it no longer seems bizarre to see the right using rhetorical weapons forged by the 19th century populist left.[61]

In 2019 the anti-statist, programme-slashing animus that drove the 1970s and 1980s tax revolt is still widely felt among Republican legislators,[62] and was a staple of the party's 2016 presidential nominee.[63] After passing a huge tax cut late in 2017, balancing the budget no longer concerns Congressional Republicans,[64] unless it can be used to justify sweeping reductions in welfare state programmes.[65] American conservatives owe Howard Jarvis a great debt, the ideological microfoundations of which are located in his campaign's use of a set of core, adjacent and peripheral concepts, conveyed in an innovative flurry of compelling representative claims.

Direct democracy and tax reform in the Reform Party of Canada

The Reform Party of Canada was formed in 1986, largely at the initiative of its founding and only leader, Preston Manning. Manning's father had been Premier of Alberta from 1944–1968, leading the right populist Social Credit League of Alberta with a combination of antagonism towards the developing Canadian welfare state and evangelical Christianity. By 1986 Preston Manning realized that the federal Progressive Conservative government's popularity among conservative voters in western Canada was sinking fast for various reasons, prominent among which was non-delivery of promised balanced budgets and major tax cuts.

The Reform Party's 1993 election breakthrough owed much to its opposition to the Charlottetown Accord. The Accord was the Progressive Conservative government's second attempt to amend the Canadian constitution to include Quebec as a signatory to the Constitution Act of 1982. The Accord was supported by all three major parties in Parliament, all provincial legislatures, big business, the establishment media and major Aboriginal leaders.[66] To ensure its legitimacy, the federal government held a national referendum vote. The Reform Party leapt at the opportunity to reject this bad 'elite deal' on behalf of 'the people'. They argued that the Accord would burden 'ordinary Canadians' with unnecessary over-governance and increased taxes. It would give more powers to Quebec's government, give more representational rights to women and Aboriginal people, produce a more complicated set of linguistic rights, and sanction a 'social and economic union' section[67] to constitutionally entrench key aspects of the Canadian welfare state.[68]

The Reform Party's opposition to the Accord displayed adjacent conceptual opposition to various forms of minority rights, and to taxation levels supporting welfare state programmes. This opposition expressed a core conceptual concern with elite rule by 'special interests' within the Canadian polity and through the three main Canadian political parties. Opposition to 'special interests' decontested its core conceptualization of the people/elite antagonism. The party did more than any other group to deny the 'Yes' side a victory in the national referendum.[69] Among its high-profile opponents, only the Reform Party and the separatist Bloc Québecois emerged from this battle with more gains than losses.

This referendum campaign polarized opinion, exacerbated alienation from parties and featured a successful test run by the Reform Party in populist demonization of 'special interests' and established political parties. This eventually evolved into a broader attack on and identification of special interests: Quebec, Aboriginal peoples, feminists, unions, and most groups benefiting from the modest Canadian welfare state.[70] Claims about the over-representation of minority voices in Canadian politics implied a representative claim on behalf of 'ordinary Canadians' who were not part of these groups, and a kind of negative definition of 'the people'. As the party said in a federal election campaign pamphlet the following year, 'In Ottawa, every special interest group counts except one: Canadians.'

On the heels of its referendum victory, and with a newly established legitimacy as the defender of 'the people', the Reform Party's populist critique took aim at 'old-line parties' and unaccountable federal politicians in the 1993 federal election. Preston Manning and RPC candidates began holding up posters at public events that said 'So you don't trust politicians? Neither do we.' The party ramped up its promotion of direct democratic end-runs around corrupt old party politicians, and portrayed existing policy development processes as the stronghold of well-positioned special interests. This case employed adjacent concepts criticizing Canadian governance as essentially corrupt and asserting the out-sized political power of groups that bribed establishment political parties with votes. Representative claims on behalf of the victims of this corrupt governance system invoked 'the common sense of the common people,' one of leader Manning's favourite sayings.[71]

Manning and the Reform party defined the special interest antagonists of 'the people' in almost exactly the same terms that Reagan and Jarvis had in California during the 1970s. Their populism turned on depicting special interest/elites as actors, organizations and groups who promoted or benefited from state intervention in the market distribution of social and economic goods, all at the people's expense. In a variety of folksy appeals in favour of equal treatment of all citizens, and against state-sponsored, tax-funded 'special rights' for privileged groups, the party attacked feminist lobby groups, native organizations, private and public sector unions, multicultural and ethnic groups, and managers of state agencies.[72] This was a largely derivative political narrative, but for many conservative Canadian voters, it became a compelling populist story about representational failure. It asserted a powerful view of equal opportunity, in Hayekian fashion, as equality under the law. This modified mirror image of left-wing equality of opportunity stripped the left-wing variant of any redistributive capacity, and functioned as a key adjacent concept in the Reform Party's ideology. It informed a range of the party's prominent peripheral concepts, policy positions objecting to special rights associated with multiculturalism, ethnicity, aboriginal status, gender, sexual orientation and disability.

The 1993 Reform Party campaign did not emphasize tax cuts, though it did stress balanced budgets, 'tax fairness', a flat tax, and spending restraint. Party leaders and strategists did not believe their party could break into the system by highlighting the new right anti-tax message.[73] Direct democracy received more attention in the party's 1993 platform, which presented the case against unaccountable party elites and for an antidote to representational failure through direct democracy:

> We believe that public policy in democratic societies should reflect the will of the majority of the citizens as determined by free and fair elections, referendums, and the decisions of legally constituted and representative Parliaments and Assemblies elected by the people. We believe in the common sense of the common people, their right to be consulted on public policy matters before major decisions are made, their right to choose and recall their own representatives and to govern themselves through truly representative and responsive institutions, and their right to directly initiate legislation for which substantial public support is demonstrated. We believe in accountability of elected representatives to the people who elect them, and that the duty of elected members to their constituents should supersede their obligations to their political parties.[74]

Preston Manning's typically restrained language here lacks the colour and bombast typical of Jarvis in full flight, yet Reform's case emphasized direct democracy for 'the people'/'the majority' even more forcefully. With the constitutional referendum campaign victory still fresh, it was time to show the 'old line parties' that voters would no longer be taken for suckers. The Reform Party aimed to mobilize high levels of anti-party sentiment in a way established parties could not.[75] Making anti-partyism a high-profile adjacent concept within the RPC's public appeal did much to attract western Canadian voters. As the party's unofficial organ reported during the election campaign,

> Reformers are calling for 'direct democracy,' a series of measures such as MP recall and citizen – initiated referendum, that put the ultimate control over the political system in the hands of ordinary Canadians. ... Reformer Johnston argues, 'Without direct democracy to ensure the ultimate power rests with the people, the small elites in this country will continue to run things as they always have.'[76]

The Reform Party entered the Canadian federal party system with a bang in the 1993 election, displacing the ruling Progressive Conservative Party as the viable party of the right in English Canada. It won 52 seats in Parliament to the Progressive Conservatives' 2 seats with 'The West wants in' as its slogan.

Between the 1993 and 1997 elections, the Reform Party contended that a range of issues should be put directly to a popular vote. They included 'issues which change Canada's basic social fabric', such as 'immigration, language and measurement'[77]; 'issues of personal conscience, such as 'abortion and capital punishment'; Aboriginal land claim and self-government agreements[78]; and federal government decisions to run deficits or raise taxes.[79] The new right proposal to discipline government budgeting with direct democracy was thus imported from the US with little fanfare, and was a significant dimension of the party's adjacent conceptual decontestation of direct democracy. It also provided a democratic legitimation for the party's preferred policies, situated as peripheral concepts in the overall ideology's morphology.

In the wake of the 1994 Republican 'Contract with America' promises for flat taxation, severe spending limits and a balanced budget amendment, the Reform party's fiscal conservatism came to the fore. By 1996, Grover Norquist's Americans for Tax Reform's 'Tax Pledge'[80] was attracting many Republican candidates' signatures. Both the 'Contract' and 'the Pledge' could trace their origins to Proposition 13. Confident that Canadian voters had a similar appetite for attacks on untrustworthy politicians, the Reform Party built its 1997 platform around a series of 'guarantees'. There were promises of major cuts to capital gains taxes and high-income surtaxes, along with a package of tax exemptions and credits for middle class taxpayers. If elected to power, the party guaranteed a public consultation on tax policy; if 'consensus' did not emerge in this process, a referendum on tax reform was guaranteed.[81] This explicit combination of two central adjacent concepts, direct democracy and tax reform, underpinned with an implicit characterization of other parties as untrustworthy, was their second representative claim about/promise for a 'fresh start'. The first focused on job creation resulting from major reductions in the size of government.[82]

At a deeper ideological level, the plebiscitary instruments of direct democracy appealed to Reform party leaders because they allowed citizens to shape state action from their individualized private spheres without enabling distorted mediation of their wills by organized interests' market-threatening, tax-heightening and bureaucracy-building actions.[83] Reform Party advocacy of direct democracy drew on related aspects of their core concept of freedom: the real freedom and consumer sovereignty of the marketplace. They contrasted this with repeated representative claims/adjacent concepts about the powerlessness of citizens facing unresponsive parties and systemic representational failure. This critique of conventional Canadian political representation sometimes seemed to undermine the very idea of representation – as opposed to 'direct' control of policy by citizens. But it was part of a broader representative claim, in which the Reform Party presented itself as the voice of the 'common sense of the common people'. In doing so the party effectively linked citizen frustration with politics to alternative ideological themes and objectives, across a range of adjacent and peripheral concepts and representative claims.

The Reform Party of Canada's intertwining of tax revolt and direct democracy promotion bore some resemblance to that of the Proposition 13 campaign, but also had some notable differences. 'Market freedom' was given a higher profile because one of the RPC's key early audiences was disgruntled right-wing voters for the incumbent Progressive Conservative government. As with business conservatives across North America, this decontestation of freedom had core conceptual weight. The argument regarding popular sovereignty and representational failure was more central to the RPC case than to Proposition 13's because the intention was to break into and exercise power within a party system, not just reduce taxes or shrink the state. This gave popular sovereignty and representational failure prominent adjacent conceptual status in their ideological morphology.

Equality defined as equal application of the rule of law was key to the RPC ideology, and enjoyed an enhanced adjacent conceptual status because of its strategic, 'mirror-imaging' character.[84] In response to the political success of centre-left understandings of equality by the mid-1980s in Canada, RPC leaders rejected any version of equality that could justify re-distributive programmes and 'group rights' that stood in the way of their desired minimalist state.[85] And a strong western regionalist anti-centralism provided a key early dimension of the party's definition of both 'the people' and its 'elite' antagonists. It also shaped a decisive RPC adjacent concept, which offered a Canadian twist on the new right ideological orientation. This built on a century-long popular democratic tradition of western populism[86] and regional alienation, and provided solid foundations for representative claims like 'the West wants in.' This anti-centralism was, however, easily woven into accounts of the representational failure inherent in an overreaching, intrusive federal state, another negatively framed adjacent concept. This image of predatory central government appealed especially effectively in western Canada, which had experienced a century of opposition to domination of federal parliamentary politics by representatives from Ontario and Quebec.

As in the Proposition 13 case, however, direct democracy fitted perfectly into the package of representative claim-making by the Reform Party, provided a valuable adjacent concept, and vindicated the new right argument concerning representational failure and diminished citizen-taxpayer freedom. It presented a rhetorical club for Reform leaders to remind voters why they distrusted politicians and 'old-line parties,' and a means through which the people's policy preferences could override those of corrupt politicians and 'special interest' elites.

A steady stream of audience-constructing representative claims from the Reform Party sought to lead 'the people' to see new right nostrums as their own preferences. The core populist conceptualization of 'the people' and 'the elite' was fashioned from the resources of recent American right-wing populism, Hayek's portrait of 'special interests' undermining the natural market order, and a healthy dose of western Canadian regionalist rejection of national government policy initiatives. Strategically, advocating direct democracy demonstrated the value of un-mediated, market-like expressions of the people's will. Such advocacy also rallied the people, as subject and audience of the RPC's representative claims, against both the special interests and the high-tax regime these interests had constructed for their own benefit. The Reform Party thus combined carefully strategic representative claims, an anti-statist definition of the people, promotion of a new right policy agenda and direct democracy advocacy to construct a distinctive right populist conceptual morphology.

By the 2000 federal election the Reform party had re-branded itself as the Canadian Conservative and Reform Alliance; in 2004 the Alliance party merged with the

Progressive Conservative Party to create the Conservative Party. With the autocratic Stephen Harper at the helm of the new party, talk of direct democracy vanished. What remained was a more conventional party strikingly dominated by its leader, no talk of systemic representational failure, and tax and programme cuts as the instruments of greater market freedom.

Populist rhetorical presentation of tax reform and state shrinkage, and an attack on 'special interests', continued even after the Conservatives formed a government in 2006. The key components of this later message were presented in an array of party pronouncements, press releases and even Budget Speeches.[87] Announcing his party's promise of a 'Tax Lock' law during the 2015 election campaign, Prime Minister Harper explained that his government 'believes in lowering taxes because we know that tax money belongs to Canadians, not the government. … This pledge backs our low-tax commitment with the force of the law.'[88] Twenty-two years after his old Reform Party colleagues broke into Parliament with him, the 10 year veteran Prime Minister Harper told his audience that taxation invokes a conflict between 'the people' and any government that wants their money. Even as Prime Minister, Steven Harper found it useful to go to the populist well to serve up his preferred conservative message.

Conclusion

In this paper, I have argued that blending Michael Freeden's interpretive model for ideology analysis with Michael Saward's constructivist theorization of political representation provides us with an analytical toolkit capable of revealing the complex interaction between the normative, strategic and performative elements in populist ideologies. Freeden's approach allows us to identify the conceptual microfoundations of complex ideologies. Saward provides insights into the discursive qualities of representation that eventually crystallize into the core, adjacent and peripheral concepts that constitute an ideological morphology as theorized by Freeden. Taken together, these two approaches enhance our consideration of the inter-related conceptual underpinnings, strategic decisions and performative mechanisms involved in populist discursive representation and ideological appeals. By blending the two approaches I hope to have provided a new perspective on the adoption of right-populist ideological packages and appeals by North American politicians in the late 20th century.

The complementary value of Freeden and Saward's approaches to understanding the conceptual morphology of and representative claims in these populisms suggests that it is a mistake to separate substantive from strategic components in analysing ideologies. The main concepts in Freeden's core, adjacent and perimeter conceptual structure are also distillates of past representative claims, which are always made strategically. And the strategic delivery mechanisms of direct democracy, charismatic leadership and various aspects of representational failure critique derive their legitimacy from the substantive rationale provided by core and adjacent concepts.

While we benefit as analysts from integrating Freeden's focus on the conceptual substance of ideology with Saward's focus on discursive representational process, neither the audience nor the communicators of ideologies disaggregate content and process in this way. For example, appealing to 'the people' as besieged taxpayers always comes with a substantive claim about the desirability of a smaller state that affords the people more liberty. Effective transmission of key ideological themes involves presentation of a package that integrates strategy, appeal and process with more basic ideological commitments.

Since the late 1970s, the popularity of direct democracy across North America has been aided by an analogy between the market, which enables consumer sovereignty, and direct democratic instruments, which allow unmediated registration of the people's will. For both the Reform Party and the Proposition 13 campaign, this analogy challenged the legitimacy of existing parties and channels of representation in the policy process. The analogy also worked in the other direction for Jarvis, the Reform Party and their ideological successors, to legitimize the extension of the market mechanism into more aspects of economic and social life.

Direct democracy and attacks on representational failure were valuable to the American and then the Canadian political right in shifting the political agenda to focus on tax cuts and state shrinkage. Riding a populist Trojan horse decorated with representative claims for the people turned out very well for conservative politicians. However, sustaining political momentum for this agenda over the past two decades seems only to have required a populist argument about representational failure. The same 'special interests' are tagged with responsibility for the people's woes, in which their tax burdens are still alleged to be central.[89]

Now that tax reform can be delivered by conservative legislators, direct democracy is dispensable to many conservative strategists, whose representative claims still portray the Republican and Conservative parties as trustworthy agents of the people's will for even lower taxes. Two generations after Jarvis, President Trump successfully promised to be the voice of the people while proposing tax cuts, despite the widely circulated warning that these would exacerbate social inequality. In a way that might both surprise and gratify right-populist pioneers Howard Jarvis and Preston Manning, Trump did this without breathing a word about direct democracy. Yet however much the culture wars and immigration fears dominate Donald Trump's rallies and tweets, populist attacks on unresponsive elites remain essential to positioning tax cuts at the centre of the North American conservative agenda.

There is considerable historical irony in the way right-wing populist arguments about freedom-crushing elites have been used to undermine the restraints on corporate power that earlier left-wing populists in the US and Canada did so much to establish. The irony underscores not just the political right's successful appropriation of populist ideological weaponry, but also the emptiness of populist concepts of 'the people' and 'elite' prior to their political contestation.[90] To appreciate the discursive intricacies and political implications of this irony, we are well advised to examine the microfoundations of this contest through the complementary analytical lenses of Freeden's conceptual morphology and Saward's representative claim.

Notes

1. For Oliver and Rahn, the 'representation gap' occurs 'when existing political parties are not responding to the desires of large sections of the electorate.' J. E. Oliver and W. M. Rahn, 'Rise of the *Trumpenvolk*: Populism in the 2016 Election', *Annals of the American Academy of Political and Social Science* 667:1 (2016), pp. 189–206; 194.

IDEOLOGIES IN ACTION

2. See, among others, C. Mudde and C. R. Kaltewasser, *Populism: A Very Short Introduction* (Oxford: Oxford University Press, 2017); D. Caramani, 'Will vs. Reason: The Populist and Technocratic forms of Political Representation and Their Critique to Party Government', *American Political Science Review* 111:1 (2017), pp. 54–67; N. Urbinati, 'Populism and the Principle of Majority', in C.R. Kaltwasser, P. Taggart, P.O. Espejo and P. Ostiguy (Eds.) *The Oxford Handbook of Populism* (Oxford: Oxford University Press, 2017); J-W Müeller, *What is Populism?* (Philadelphia: University of Pennsylvania Press, 2016); B. Moffitt, *The Global Rise of Populism: Performance, Political Style and Representation.* (Stanford: Stanford University Press, 2016); K. Abts and S. Rummens, 'Populism vs. Democracy,' *Political Studies* 55:2 (2007), pp. 405–424; B. Arditi, 'Populism as an internal periphery of democratic politics', in F. Panizza (Ed.) *Populism and the Mirror of Democracy* (London: Verso 2005); E. Lacalu, *On Populist Reason* (London: Verso 2005); M. Canovan, 'Populism for Political Theorists?' *Journal of Political Ideologies* 9:3 (2004), pp. 241–52 and P. Taggart, 'Populism and the pathology of representative politics', in Y. Mény and Y. Surel (Eds.) *Democracies and the populist challenge* (New York: Palgrave, 2002).

3. M. Freeden, *Ideologies and Political Theory* (Oxford: Oxford University Press, 1996) and M. Freeden, *The Political Theory of Political Thinking* (Oxford: Oxford University Press, 2013) .

4. M. Saward, *The Representative Claim* (Oxford: Oxford University Press, 2010); and M. Saward, 'Shape-shifting Representation', *American Political Science Review* 108:4 (2014), pp. 723–36.

5. E. Laclau (2005), *op. cit.* Ref. 2; C. Mudde and C. K. Rovira, eds., *Populism in Europe and the Americas: Threat or Corrective for Democracy?* (New York: Cambridge University Press, 2012).

6. Freeden (1996), op. cit., Ref. 3, pp. 333–34.

7. M. Freeden, 'Editorial: ideological boundaries and ideological systems', *Journal of Political Ideologies*, 8:1 (2003), pp. 3–12; 13.

8. Both Mudde and Kaltewasser and Stanley have applied Freeden's notion of a 'thin ideology' to their analyses of populism. See C. Mudde and C. R. Kaltewasser (2017) *op. cit.*, Ref. 2; B. Stanley, 'The thin ideology of populism', *Journal of Political Ideologies* 13: 1 (2008), pp. 95–110. More recently, Michael Freeden has argued that most current European populisms are not complex and nuanced enough to qualify as 'thin-centred' ideologies. Freeden suggests the descriptor 'phantom ideologies' to characterize populisms, due to their amorphous, sporadic and contagious nature, and populist politicians' intentional blurring and concealing during public discussion of 'pressing and intricate socio-political issues' (Freeden, 'After the Brexit referendum: revisiting populism as an ideology', *Journal of Political Ideologies* 22:1 (2017), pp. 1–11.).

9. See Oliver and Rahn (2016), *op. cit.*, Ref. 1, and authors referred to in endnote 2 earlier.

10. See, for example, D. Laycock, 'Visions of Popular Sovereignty: Mapping the Contested Terrain of Contemporary Western Populisms', *Critical Review of International Social and Political Philosophy* 8:1 (2005), pp. 125–144.

11. This is stressed in, among others, Y. Mény and Y. Surel, 'The constitutive ambiguity of populism', in Y. Mény and Y. Surel (eds), *Democracies and the Populist Challenge* (Oxford: Palgrave Macmillan, 2002); P. Taggart (2002), *op. cit.*, Ref. 2; E. Laclau (2005), op. cit., Ref. 2; B. Moffitt (2016), op. cit., Ref. 2, and Y. Stavrakakis (2014), 'The Return of "the People": Populism and Anti-Populism in the Shadow of the European Crisis', *Constellations* 21:4 (2014), pp. 505–517.

12. See M. Saward, 'Authenticity and Authorization', *The Journal of Political Philosophy*, 17 (2008), pp. 1–22, and Saward (2010), op. cit., Ref. 4.

13. Saward (2010), *ibid.*, p. 36.

14. Saward (2010), *ibid.*, p. 36.

15. Saward, (2014) op. cit., Ref. 4.

16. Full Text: Donald Trump 2016 RNC draft speech transcript, *Politico* 21 July 2016, https://www.politico.com/story/2016/07/full-transcript-donald-trump-nomination-acceptance-speech-at-rnc-225974.

17. B. Bonikowski and N. Gidron, 'The Populist Style in American Politics: Presidential Campaign Discourse, 1952–1996', *Social Forces*, 94 (2016): 1593–1621; 1605.
18. B. Bonikowski and N. Gidron, 'Populism in Legislative Discourse: Evidence from the European Parliament, 1999–2004'. Working paper, Harvard University, Cambridge MA, 2016, p. 3.
19. C. Mudde and C.R. Kaltwasser, *op. cit.*, Ref. 2; D. Laycock, (2005), op. cit., Ref. 10.
20. For a clear articulation of this by an influential movement conservative, see R. Viguerie, *The establishment vs. the people: is a new populist revolt on the way?* (Chicago: Regnery Gateway, 1983).
21. Freeden (2013), op. cit., Ref. 3, pp. 285–86.
22. See B. Moffitt (2016), op. cit., Ref. 2, ch. 7.
23. Several promising investigations of 'populist political communication' have recently been published which offer alternate ways of appreciating the connection between conceptual structure, performance and representative claiming in populist ideology. See especially T. Aalberg, F. Esser, C. Reinemann, J. Strömbäck and C. de Vreese, eds., *Populist Political Communication in Europe* (London: Routledge, 2017), and M. Hameleers, L. Bos and C. de Vreese, 'They Did It': The Effects of Emotionalized Blame Attribution in Populist Communication', *Communication Research* 44: 6 (2017), pp. 870–900.
24. For more insight on this, see Saward (2010), op. cit., Ref. 4, and L. Disch, 'Towards a Mobilization Conception of Representation', *American Political Science Review*, 105:1 (2011), pp. 100–114.
25. Saward (2014) op. cit., Ref. 4 stresses the multiple and potentially inconsistent roles played by makers of representative claims. For an insightful account of the importance of performance, broadly construed, to the presentation and success of populist ideologies, see B. Moffitt (2016), op. cit., Ref 2.
26. Saward (2014), ibid., p. 727.
27. See D. Barney and D. Laycock, 'Right-Populists and Plebiscitary Politics in Canada', *Party Politics*, 5:2 (1999), pp. 317–339.
28. Saward (2014), op. cit., Ref. 4, p. 731.
29. This connection among variants of populist ideology, rhetoric, communication style and organization is creatively explored by M. Caiani and P.R. Graziano, 'Varieties of populism: insights from the Italian case', *Italian Political Science Review* (2016), pp. 1–25. B. Moffitt (2016), op. cit., Ref. 2, does a particularly good job of analyzing the connections between ideology, performance and modes of representation.
30. See Laycock (2005), op. cit., Ref. 10, and the references listed in endnote 2 earlier.
31. Saward (2014), op. cit., Ref. 4, 733–34.
32. Hannah Pitkin showed over 50 years ago that almost all modern political actors attempt to present their actions as legitimate because representative of the people's will or the public interest. H. Pitkin, *The Concept of Representation* (Berkeley: University of California Press, 1967).
33. See Saward (2010), *op. cit.*, Ref. 4, ch. 6, for an account of how such reception provides representative claims with a measure of democratic legitimacy.
34. V. Williamson, 'Tax me. Please', *New York Times*, 8 October 2016.
35. See Goldwater's *Conscience of a Conservative* (1960), especially chs. 7 and 8, and C. Mohr, 'Goldwater Gives a Tax-cut Pledge', *New York Times*, 6 September 1964, at http://www.nytimes.com/1964/09/06/goldwater-gives-a-taxcut-pledge.html?_r=0.
36. I. Martin, 'How Republicans Learned to Sell Tax Cuts for the Rich', *New York Times* 18 December 2017, accessed on December 20 at https://www.nytimes.com/2017/12/18/opinion/republicans-tax-cuts-rich.html?&moduleDetail=section-news-2&action=click&contentCollection=Opinion&region=Footer&module=MoreInSection&version=WhatsNext&contentID=WhatsNext&pgtype=article.
37. R. Reagan, 'Reflections on the Failure of Proposition #1', *National Review*, December 1973. http://www.nationalreview.com/article/210999/reflections-failure-proposition-1-governor-ronald-reagan.

39. My account of the Proposition 13 campaign is based on visits to the Institute for Governmental Studies Library at the University of California, Berkeley, and the California State Library in Sacramento, in November 2015. Sources included newspaper files, pamphlets, academic and media commentaries and the personal papers of Howard Jarvis and Paul Gann.

38. See M. Klausner, 'Inside Ronald Reagan', *Reason*, July 1975, accessed 20 December 2017 at http://reason.com/archives/1975/07/01/inside-ronald-reagan.

40. See http://www.cato.org/publications/commentary/proposition-13-then-now-forever.

41. See Moffitt (2016), op. cit., Ref. 2.

42. Oliver and Rahn (2016), op. cit., Ref. 1.

43. D. Smith, 'Howard Jarvis, Populist Entrepreneur: Reevaluating the Causes of Proposition 13', *Social Science History* 23(1999), pp. 173–210.

44. For a brief primer, see Miriam Pawel, 'Ballot Initiatives are Powerful. The Powerful have noticed', *The New York Times*, 5 November 2018, at https://www.nytimes.com/2018/11/05/opinion/california-ballot-initiatives-direct-democracy.html?action=click&module=MoreInSection&pgtype=Article&region=Footer&contentCollection=Opinion.

45. E. Laclau, *Politics and Ideology in Marxist Theory* (London: Verso, 1977), ch. 4.

46. H. Jarvis, *I'm Mad as Hell* (New York: Times Books, 1979), pp. 36–40.

47. See Clyde Haberman, 'The California Ballot Measure that inspired a Tax Revolt', *New York Times*, 16 October 2016. TV news clips from the campaign are available at http://www.nytimes.com/video/us/100000004711534/proposition-13-mad-as-hell.html?action=click&contentCollection=us&module=lede&region=caption&pgtype=article.

48. Jarvis (1979), *op. cit.*, Ref. 46.

49. In 1911, Progressive California Governor Hiram Johnson secured state legislative enablement of the initiative, referendum and recall. The editor of the *Sacramento Bee*, a good friend of the Governor, opined that 'Big business, the Interests, the Southern Pacific ... the unclean and vile in politics and in social and commercial life ... these no longer dominate the halls of legislation. The money changers – the legions of Mammon and of Satan – these have been lashed out of the temple of the people.' Quoted in P. Schrag, 'Drowning Democracy: Our Century of Voter Initiatives', in *Boom: A Journal of California* (2011), 1:3, p.13.

50. Jarvis (1979), op. cit., Ref. 46, p. 125.

51. Freeden (1996) *op. cit.*, Ref. 3, p. 334.

52. See in particular M. Kazin, *The Populist Persuasion.* (Ithaca: Cornell University Press, 1998).

53. D. Sears and J. Citrin, *Tax Revolt: Something for Nothing in California.* (Cambridge, MA: Harvard University Press, 1982).

54. J. Ross, 'What has Proposition 13 Meant for California'? *California Voter: The League of Women Voters*, (Spring 1998), pp. 10–14; P. Schrag, (2011), op. cit., Ref. 49, pp. 13–29.

55. Proposition 62 was invalidated by the courts.

56. Proposition 218 imposed referendum requirements on all general local tax increases and a 2/3 vote requirement on all special purpose taxes, while prohibiting school districts from imposing taxes. Ross (1998), *op. cit.*, Ref. 54.

57. See, for example, R. Perlstein *The Invisible Bridge: The Fall of Nixon and the Rise of Reagan.* (New York: Simon and Shuster, 2014).

58. Reagan commented in a syndicated column that 'the news of Jarvis's success [in collecting enough signatures] was barely out when the special interests that gourmandize at the public trough began howling.' R. Reagan, 'Great Tax Revolt', (1978) *Long Beach Independent Press-Telegram*, np. (Jarvis Collection, California State Library, Sacramento, Boxes 1677 and 1974).

59. http://www.conservativeusa.net/hpbio.htm.

60. Howard Phillips, back cover endorsement of Richard Viguerie's influential *The Establishment Vs. The People, op cit.*, Ref. 20.

61. See, in particular, L. Goodwyn, *Democratic Promise: The Populist Moment in America* (New York: Oxford University Press, 1976).

62. The American Legislative Exchange Council has drawn up model legislation for state legislatures to press for a federal constitutional amendment and promoted another such run at constitutional change. See https://www.alec.org/model-policy/alecs-balanced-budget-amendment-policy/ and http://bba4usa.org/.

63. Donald Trump listed tax reform as the first component of his 'economic vision', at https://www.donaldjtrump.com/policies/tax-plan/, accessed 12 May 2016.

64. P. Krugman, 'Budgets, Bad Faith and 'Balance', *New York Times* 18 February 2018, accessed February 18 at https://www.nytimes.com/2018/02/15/opinion/republicans-bad-faith-krugman.html?rref=collection%2Fcolumn%2Fpaul-krugman&action=click&contentCollection=opinion&region=stream&module=stream_unit&version=latest&contentPlacement=7&pgtype=collection.

65. J. Stein, 'Ryan says Republicans to target welfare, Medicare, Medicaid spending in 2018', *Washington Post* 6 December 2017, accessed December 10 at https://www.washingtonpost.com/news/wonk/wp/2017/12/01/gop-eyes-post-tax-cut-changes-to-welfare-medicare-and-social-security/?utm_term=.12b5fa9df1a6.

66. Five years after the referendum, Canadian Prime Minister Stephen Harper told a conservative American think-tank conference that 'this constitutional proposal was supported by the entire Canadian political establishment ... all of the major media. ... the three largest traditional parties ... very vocally by all of the major CEOs of the country [and] the leading labour unions. ... And most academics. And it was defeated ... [by] a rag-tag opposition of a few dissident conservatives and a few dissident socialists.' Speech to Council on National Policy, June 1997, Montreal. http://www.cbc.ca/canadavotes2006/leadersparties/harper_speech.html. See also https://cfnp.org/.

67. http://www.thecanadianencyclopedia.ca/en/article/charlottetown-accord-document/#h3_jump_12.

68. T. Flanagan, *Waiting for the Wave: Preston Manning and the Reform Party of Canada* (Montreal: McGill-Queen's University Press, 1995); D. Laycock, *The New Right and Democracy in Canada: Understanding Reform and the Canadian Alliance* (Toronto: Oxford University Press, 2001).

69. R. Johnston, A. Blais, E. Gidengil and N. Nevitte, *The Challenge of Direct Democracy: The 1992 Canadian Referendum* (Montreal: McGill-Queens University Press, 1996).

70. Laycock (2001), op. cit., Ref. 68.

71. See E.P. Manning, *The New Canada* (Toronto: Macmillan, 1991), and Reform Party of Canada, *Blue Sheet: Principles, Policies and Election Platform* (Calgary, 1993).

72. D. Barney and D. Laycock (1999), op. cit., Ref. 27, p. 324. The Reform Party's account of the special interests manipulating the political system was ideologically remote from earlier populist promotion of direct democracy in Canada. From 1910 to 1921, various farmer and labour organizations presented direct democracy as a means of reducing the power of corporate interests and their old party 'agents'. D. Laycock, *Populism and Democratic Thought in the Canadian Prairies: 1910–1945* (Toronto: University of Toronto Press, 1990).

73. Flanagan (1995), op. cit., Ref. 68.

74. Reform Party of Canada (1993), op. cit., Ref. 71, p. 3.

75. E. Bélanger, 'Anti-partyism and Third party vote choice', *Comparative Political Studies* 37:9 (2004), pp. 1054–1078.

76. Western Report, 'Let the people decide: the RPC (Reform Party of Canada) stands alone in demanding that ruling elites relinquish their stranglehold on power', *Western Report*, 20 September 1993, pp. 16–17.

77. Visible minority immigration, official bilingualism and conversion from Imperial to metric measurement were hot button issues for many Reform party members, who believed that 'Eastern elites' had forced all of these 'changes to Canada's basic social fabric' down the throats of ordinary people. Opposition to non-white immigration among Reform party voters was markedly higher than among all other party voters, and between 2004 and 2015 a large gap remained on this issue between Conservative party voters and all other party supporters.

IDEOLOGIES IN ACTION

78. For an account of the Reform party's opposition to 'native rights' and multiculturalism, see Laycock (2001), op. cit., Ref. 68, ch. 4.
79. Reform Party of Canada, *Blue Sheet: Principles and Policies* (Calgary, Alberta: 1996).
80. http://abcnews.go.com/blogs/politics/2012/11/norquists-tax-pledge-what-it-is-and-how-it-started/.
81. Reform Party of Canada, *A Fresh Start for Canadians: 1997 Reform party Platform.* (Calgary, Alberta: 1997), p. 11.
82. Reform Party of Canada (1997), *ibid.*, pp. 6–9.
83. Barney and Laycock (1999), op. cit., Ref. 27, p. 326.
84. Freeden (1996), *op cit.*, Ref. 3, p. 336.
85. For details, see Laycock (2001), *op. cit.*, Ref. 68.
86. These were treated as such in Manning (1991), *op. cit.*, Ref. 71, and in the party's early manifestos.
87. D. Laycock, 'Populism and Democracy in Canada's Reform Party', ch. 11 in Mudde and Rovira (2012), op. cit., Ref. 2.
88. http://www.conservative.ca/prime-minister-harper-announces-new-tax-lock-law/ (September 25). This announcement was posted immediately to Conservative party candidates' websites.
89. I. Martin, *Rich People's Movements: Grass Roots Campaigns to Un-tax the 1%.* (New York: Oxford University Press, 2013).
90. E. Laclau (2005), op. cit., Ref. 2. Laclau presents 'the people' as both the central populist concept and as an 'empty signifier' par excellence, the most open to discursive appropriation and use as a powerful ideological tool.

Acknowledgments

This work was supported by the Social Sciences and Humanities Research Council of Canada with a Connections Development Grant, number 611-2015-0386, and by Simon Fraser University.

Disclosure statement

No potential conflict of interest was reported by the author.

Inventing America, *again*

Howard Brick

ABSTRACT

In US intellectual and academic life, the 1940s and 1950s stand out as a period abounding with attempts to assay the characteristic and distinctive forms of 'American culture' and 'American society,' from Gunnar Myrdal's *An American Dilemma* and the oft-noted 'Tocqueville revival' to works by Harold Laski, Max Lerner, David Riesman, C. L. R. James, the 'consensus historians,' and the early writers in the field of American Studies. Viewed as the culmination of a half-century span (roughly 1900–1950) of cultural nation-building, this rush of 'American' definitions at mid-century was shot through with politics – but in complex ways that are not adequately captured by the familiar recourse to Cold War anticommunism as the presumed ideological bedrock of the time. By treating this cultural nationalism as the outcome of an uneven and combined intellectual-historical process, we see how elusive (and illusory) the enterprise of designating 'American' traits actually was.

'In short, by 1945, America having won a war on both her oceans, and finding herself involved in the four quarters of the earth, was quite simply *the* world power, which means: the center of world awareness: it was Europe that was provincial.'

–Jacques Barzun, 'Our Country and Our Culture,' 1952[1]

'Look at me, going everywhere! Why, I am a sort of Columbus of those near-at-hand and believe you can come to them in this immediate *terra incognita* that spreads out in every gaze. I may well be a flop at this line of endeavor. Columbus too thought he was a flop, probably, when they sent him back in chains. Which didn't prove there was no America.'

–Saul Bellow, *The Adventures of Augie March*, 1953[2]

'America does not exist. I know. I've been there.'

–*Mon oncle d'Amerique* (1980)[3]

Francis Otto Matthiessen, known as the eminent literary scholar F. O. Matthiessen and as 'Matty' to his friends, was in his forties during the 1940s. Born 1902 in the Midwest, Matthiessen had gone through Yale (joining its most elite club, Skull and Bones) and then went on, for a Ph.D. and a professorship, to Harvard, where he published his masterwork, *American Renaissance: Art and Expression in Age of Emerson and Whitman*, in 1941. A large book treating only five writers in depth – Emerson, Thoreau, Hawthorne, Melville and Whitman – this study, Matthiessen stated at the outset, did *not* mean to describe the literary work of two decades, from 1836 to 1855, as 'a re-birth of values that had existed previously in America, but as America's way of producing a renaissance, by coming to its first maturity and affirming its rightful heritage in the whole expanse of art and culture.'[4] Matthiessen's diction was all about American belonging: he sought to understand 'the concentrated abundance of *our* mid-nineteenth century' through the medium of those 'conceptions held by ... *our* major writers concerning the function and nature of literature.'[5] And he was self-conscious about his method, which was to be holistic, capturing the 'whole movement' of the 'general culture' during the period he studied by plumbing the role of *myth* – not something false but something taken as legendary that lies at the foundation of experience in any age, 'the primal vitality of the stories that are preserved in the popular memory' – and of *symbol* or image recurring in diverse arts, such as 'the open air' that poets, landscape painters, or the new photographers saw as their medium.[6] There are good reasons to see Matthiessen as the source of a method, known as 'myth-symbol' analysis, which set the standard of a new discipline, American Studies, which had its own journal, *American Quarterly*, beginning in 1949.

Two writers later renowned as that method's leading practitioners – Henry Nash Smith and Leo Marx – had been Harvard students and colleagues of Matthiessen's in the late 1930s. Marx edited the *Harvard Progressive*, a journal associated with left-wing students and with the Teachers Union, led by Matthiessen and enrolling young faculty sharing the students' affiliation with the Popular Front, that milieu of radicals and liberals who rallied to support the New Deal, fight all manifestations of fascism abroad and at home, and back the power of the Soviet Union as the centre of anti-fascist forces in the world at large. In that milieu, Matthiessen collaborated with Communist Party activists even though he never joined the party himself, holding to principles quite his own. He regularly described himself as a socialist and a Christian – as an American went without saying. His Christianity entailed convictions comprised too in his socialism (devotion to human equality and brotherly love) along with recognition of the evil that dwelled within such fallen creatures as ourselves; in that respect, Matthiessen embraced a 'tragic sense of life' that he saw in such men of faith as Kierkegaard and the neo-orthodox theologian Karl Barth.[7] And, thus, the mood that characterized *American Renaissance* was buoyant in its affirmation of values Matthiessen deemed characteristically American – fresh as a springtime rebirth – but also measured. He intended the book as an 'effort to repossess ... the total pattern' of his five writers' achievement – a 'literature for our democracy ... [composed in] our first great age,' so that 'we can [again] feel the challenge of our still undiminished resources.'[8] He loved Whitman, but he saw the 'tragic sense of life' in Hawthorne and above all in Melville. Emerson championed the ability to make the world new but was limited by over-confidence in 'the increasing greatness of man'; Matthiessen cherished Thoreau's mastery of 'organic form,' the discovery in nature and in prose of 'wholeness,' but he remained ambivalent about Thoreau's 'anarchical basis.' It was Melville's 'reckoning with ... as much suffering and evil as he had seen' that granted to the novelist what Matthiessen admired most, that is, access to 'his own undissevered experience.'[9]

Matthiessen had just a bit of the American missionizing spirit too. After the war's end, he collaborated with Harvard students who established the Salzburg Seminar in American Studies – in occupied Austria – with the hope of offering Europe 'something on the plane of ideas, scholarship, culture' to complement US aid for 'material reconstruction.'[10] Matthiessen was the premier lecturer at the first Salzburg Seminar in the summer of 1947. He was eager to spend time overseas, not out of an expatriate's desire to get away but rather, as he wrote in the 1948 book describing his travels, *From the Heart of Europe*, because 'I want to write about some of the things it means to be an American today. That is the chief thing I came to Europe to think about.'[11] To be sure, definitions of a nation's culture often depend on views from afar, whether that of a foreign visitor or of nationals travelling abroad and looking back. And so Matthiessen, who studied 'our first great age' so 'we can [again] feel the challenge of our still undiminished resources,' might have been well-equipped to hail the greatness of American culture at mid-century, as the US stood at the centre of the world. In *From the Heart of Europe*, he repeatedly noted the quantum leap in the interest European readers showed in American literature at a time when US power and influence in western Europe was paramount.

By then, however, Matthiessen appeared in the eyes of the American public as one of those deemed 'un-American,' hounded by the press as a soft-minded apologist for the country's Cold War enemy, the USSR. And then, suddenly: 'Harvard Prof Identified as Plunge Victim,' the *Chicago Daily Tribune* reported on 1 April 1950, naming the suicide as Matthiessen, who had been repeatedly smeared in that conservative newspaper's columns. Jumping from the twelfth floor of a Boston hotel, Matthiessen left a note confessing to severe depression, apologizing to his friends for his 'desperate act,' and adding at the very end a political testament: 'How much the state of the world has to do with my state of mind I do not know. But as a Christian and a socialist believing in international peace, I find myself terribly oppressed by the present tensions.'[12] Indeed, whether his desperate act should be interpreted as a sign of dread amid Cold War pressures – or ascribed purely to inconsolable personal unhappiness – was something his friends and critics debated for a long time afterward. His work nonetheless remained a landmark of scholarly Americanism, an endeavour of national self-definition in terms of the country's emblematic literary achievements. Perhaps, there is no irony in the fact that such an effort would flourish at a time when definitions of what is 'American' were in flux and, indeed, profoundly uncertain.

A method of 'uneven and combined' intellectual history

This examination of cultural Americanism at mid-century aims to challenge a certain kind of 'historicism' that unduly conflates a range of political and cultural phenomena coexisting at a particular historical moment and in so doing produces a crude 'ideological' reading of intellectual developments at that time. I hope to sketch a different approach, one highlighting 'uneven and combined development' in intellectual history, that examines ideologies – in this case, a cultural nationalism that ventures to define 'Americanness' – in more subtle ways.

An intellectual history of uneven and combined development aims to disaggregate diversely paced currents in the temporal flow of prevailing ideas. As a method, such an intellectual history seeks to characterize the peculiar, almost fortuitous ideational composites that mark a particular pass in historical experience (a snapshot in time, a view taken when contemporary or latter-day observers sense some kind of crisis or watershed in events); such an inquiry attempts thereby to penetrate and critically *unravel* terms of consciousness that *seem*, in the composite, to govern a historical moment. The critique of 'historicism' adopted here does not, of course, deride historicity, for my preferred method is deeply historical as it attempts to grasp a *moving* phenomenon (an ideational composite) in as much complexity as is possible. Rather, the 'historicism' I challenge is the notion, implied in a tradition running from Giambattista Vico's 'New Science' through the philosophy of Benedetto Croce, that imagines historical moments as integral units, a clean cross-section (as it were) in time, wherein all aspects of experience cohere in a definite pattern that, in its turn, determines the meaning of all component parts. This is, to put it simply, the historicist notion of Zeitgeist, that unitary spirit which marks a 'time' or 'age' as uniquely marked and homogeneous.[13]

The mode of intellectual history I propose, thus, challenges, for instance, the convention of viewing the American 'Fifties' as a whole through the lens of what the iconoclastic sociologist C. Wright Mills scornfully dubbed 'the great American celebration.' That is to say, retrospective observers conventionally judge the onset of the 'American Studies' movement (inspired by writers like F. O. Matthiessen) – and allied phenomena such as the so-called 'Tocqueville revival' or the proliferation of studies that aimed to define 'American civilization' – as simple creatures of the Cold War-inspired, anti-communist drive for national mobilization and morale. That kind of 'ideological' reduction – in my view a *historicist* error – not only mistakes the actual content of much intellectual work that occurred in the past; it also avoids the work of criticism that is enabled by an alternative, 'uneven and combined' approach that unravels illusory wholes. Such unravelling differs from a venture in debunking ideology as false; rather it entails a process of doubting the fixity and givenness of meanings in history, emphasizing instead a view of humans *making* history out of circumstances that are inherited and inhabited but never neatly composed as a whole.

Thus, this essay argues not only that the post-war surge of studies in Americanism cannot be reduced to Cold War-motivated morale-building but also that among significant writers on the presumably distinctive and definitive character of 'America' (in its social, cultural and political dimensions), many recognized explicitly or implicitly how *indefinite* such an object actually was. The historical discourse of what I will call 'cultural nation-building,' viewed both in its cumulative emergence over preceding decades and in the composite form it assumed after World War II, might in some ways be rescued from the condescension of posterity (signalled, for instance, by the wholesale disregard of holistic interpretations of 'American culture' within current-day American Studies)[14]: To be sure, much of the earlier literature is dubious, faulty, and even objectionable on many grounds, yet a number of participants in that Americanist discourse appear sophisticated and provocative when read with greater attention to the complexity of the scene they faced.

Phases of cultural nation-building

The story of F. O. Matthiessen is telling because he pursued a project of defining an 'American' canon of literature precisely at that moment when campaigns to combat an internal 'un-American' threat wielded considerable power in the US, a power to which he was, in some respects, subjected. He was not alone: several other exponents of 'American Studies' in the mid-twentieth century, like Leo Marx, reached their scholarly maturity just as they had reason to think they too had come under fire from the latter-day Americanizers of the red scare. This circumstance hints at the actual *torsion* of US intellectual life at this moment, a result of uneven development that I hope to unravel in this essay: At a time when world hegemony (a status in the making for decades but fully revealed and consolidated only with the conclusion of World War II) combined with global Cold War conflict to stimulate ventures in cultural nation-building, the social and political relations defining American life were actually in process of substantial change, rendering many habitual assumptions of 'American' culture and character either obsolete or subject to acute stress.

As always, what was 'American' was a moving target and attempts to pin it down proved unavailing. It was certainly the case, as historian Wendy Wall points out, that the imperative placed on defining 'the American way of life,' in any number of government-sponsored and civil-society initiatives during the 1940s and 1950s, could never reach a true consensus on what exactly 'the American way' consisted of. Every term applied to the American way – 'freedom,' 'equality,' or even 'property' – meant different things to different contenders in debate. The 'freedom' of business ideology was at odds with the personal and collective freedoms that the labour movement considered part of freedom from want; and despite the suppression of a far left and the pre-eminence of 'free enterprise' talk, the debate over kinds of freedom remained evident throughout those years.[15] In fact, the most sophisticated students of American history and culture at that time, notably those identified with such enterprises as American Studies or 'consensus' history, acknowledged explicitly or implicitly that the very object, Americanness, was by nature a variable, fleeting and fugitive thing, virtually beyond definition.

Ever since Benedict Anderson's *Imagined Communities*, we have become accustomed to the idea that nation-building entails both material and discursive construction – via transportation and communication networks that practically create dense links and interactions within a delimited territorial space as well as by the constitution of fellow-feeling through practices and ideas that spread through that space (and beyond, to comprise even those afar who identify with it). Moreover, these varied types of nation-building are perpetual. We can assume that attempts to fashion an 'American' identity, character or culture have persisted almost continuously since the mid-eighteenth century, yet we can also identify particular periods when those efforts attained a special degree of concentration and focused energy.[16] Two periods stand out – the second quarter of the nineteenth century and the first half of the twentieth – not because these times were unusually harmonious, since conflict and dissension flourished, but because social, political and intellectual conditions encouraged holistic visions and provoked varied campaigns to realize them. The 1830s and 1840s witnessed self-conscious literary campaigns declaring 'American' independence, that is, attempts to refute the idea that American culture was a provincial or peripheral phenomenon distant from but dependent on a civilization centred in Europe – whether advanced by transcendentalists or the propagandists of 'Manifest Destiny.' In contrast, a long subsequent period – the intensified sectional crisis of the 1850s, civil war, reconstruction and even much of the Gilded Age – proved relatively slack in terms of strong pretensions to unity of character, culture, national identity and purpose. A political culture still stirred by denunciations of 'rum, Romanism, and rebellion' (1884) remained part of an age of fracture.

From the mid-1890s, however, new forces – US industrial might, the embrace of extra-continental imperialism and aspirations to world leadership, the height of the new immigration, new demands on the powers of central government, and the emergence of a modern stratum of intellectuals – kicked off a general 'Americanizing' drive (using that term in a very broad sense). There was, at the start, a 'new nationalism,' to borrow Theodore Roosevelt's campaign slogan (borrowed in turn from the intellectual Herbert Croly), that was signalled by programmes, either coercive or liberal, to foster the assimilation of immigrants. It was signalled as well by the cultivation of nation-wide norms in all things, from grading meat to training physicians; and by the fashioning of national cultural canons of artistic achievement.[17] The latter trend gained steam even as intellectual life grew more cosmopolitan: The Armory Show of modern European art (1913) was not sharply divorced from the critical milieu of Van Wyck Brooks's pioneering literary history, *America's Coming of Age* (1915).[18] This general spirit persisted for decades, gaining additional fillips of energy from depression-era and wartime morale-building, even as conditions and the tenor of consciousness changed. The experience of crisis and the trend towards political centralization over the course of the 1930s and 1940s fostered a new Americanist folklore movement, mass movements of population and an ever-deeper etching of trans-regional integration. All these, by 1950, would meld with the final achievement of globalist power and a furious political reaction determined to subdue the (oft-forgotten) class struggles of 1945–47, just in time for military mobilization again, devoted now to rolling back communism in Korea.[19]

The rise of a modern stratum of intellectuals – a development coinciding with the eclipse of clerical cultural authority – proved a key element of this second great wave of cultural nation-building in the first half of the twentieth century. The traditional intellectual elite of the Protestant clergy had suffered assaults from dissenters and reformers from the antebellum period onward, but through most of the nineteenth century it nonetheless sustained its pre-eminence in ordinary civic life and in college curricula still geared towards theistic moral philosophy. Thereafter, the modern research university plus slick magazine publishing and the new age of the 'little magazine' – all reaching their first peak in the two beginning decades of the twentieth century – fostered a new phenomenon by the 1920s: secular, self-conscious 'intellectuals' whose vocation was precisely one of sensing the temper of the times and commenting on 'value' questions that once had been the province of ministers. Their advance, along with mass communications, popular culture, and ideological politics, had led by the 1950s to the evaporation of Protestant hegemony and an official 'tri-faith' (Protestant-Catholic-Jew) disposition that more or less conceded to a modernist separation of sacred/secular realms.[20]

Indeed, the current of literary criticism that led up to Matthiessen's *American Renaissance* began (by Matthiessen's own testimony) from the work of Van Wyck Brooks and allied critics, whose work was followed by the rediscovery of Herman Melville in the 1920s and the inception of serious scholarly attention to *American* literature within formerly exclusive *English* departments.[21] The first major academic publication in the field, *American Literature: A Journal of Literary History, Criticism, and Bibliography*, commenced in 1929. Tellingly, the founding editor, Jay B. Hubbell at

Duke University, compared his new quarterly to Emerson's *Dial*, drawing a link to that previous period of cultural nation-building.[22] The disenchantment with American life voiced by 'Lost Generation' writers did not interrupt this nationalizing trend, for historian Brooke Blower has demonstrated how much the expatriate experience in Paris encouraged 'becoming American' – stemming both from the fascination (and antipathy) Parisians showed for putatively 'American' styles and manners and from the American exiles' view from afar of their home country.[23] Harold Stearns's famously caustic collection of essays, *Civilization in the United States* (1922), built on Brooks's critique of the Puritan heritage in *America's Coming of Age*; in any case, Stearns wrote of his own rapprochement with home 15 years later, *America: A Reappraisal*.[24]

As it turns out, the literary scholar Perry Miller, whose magisterial mid-century studies of American Puritanism upended the negative stereotype shared by Stearns's expatriates, had been another wanderer abroad, looking for adventure in the Congo during the 1920s, when he experienced 'a sudden epiphany ... of the pressing necessity of expounding my America to the 20th century.'[25] Many of these early cultivators of American cultural studies happened to be political radicals as well as 'new' Americans of immigrant origins, such as Alfred Kazin, whose *On Native Grounds* followed Matthiessen's *American Renaissance* by only 1 year, telling the story of *modern* American literature and already, in 1941, writing Fitzgerald, Hemingway, Dos Passos, and Faulkner into a national canon.[26] (Kazin served as a lecturer at the first Salzburg Seminar in American Studies, junior to Matthiessen, and was remembered as leading a rousing chorus there of the *Internationale*.)[27] Canon-building continued apace. Faulkner was elevated to high literary status by Malcolm Cowley's 1946 edition of *The Portable Faulkner* – only one of the volumes in the Viking Portable Library that added Emerson, Thoreau, Hawthorne, Poe, Whitman and Fitzgerald to the series in one great rush from 1945 to 1948. Melville's inclusion had to wait until 1952 and Henry James's until 1956.

Tellingly, Perry Miller (writing retrospectively about his Congo epiphany) described his mission as expounding 'the *innermost propulsion* of the US' and began with the Puritan tradition because he sought 'a coherence with which I could coherently begin.'-[28] Indeed, a determinedly holistic method marked the culmination of cultural nation-building by 1950, drawing on principles established by that time in key disciplines such as anthropology and sociology. The understanding of 'culture as a whole way of life,' as Raymond Williams famously put it in *Culture and Society* (1958), was (as Williams recognized) already the keystone of Franz Boas's cultural pluralism. That method was reinforced by the 'culture and personality' studies by Boas's acolytes Ruth Benedict and Margaret Mead, begun in the 1930s and applied to the cultures of modern nation-states during and after World War II – notwithstanding Boas's own deep suspicion of the conformism fostered by modern nationalisms.[29] The holistic disposition marked as well the sociological theory of Talcott Parsons, almost regnant in the 1940s and 1950s, given its insistence that societies (of which modern nations were one sort, and the sort that most interested Parsons) cohered due to a 'system' of 'shared values' that knitted social action together into an intricate web.

All these trends keyed a *centred* notion of society, culture and nation – that is, the assumption that these could be understood as bounded entities each built around some kind of 'innermost' principle or pattern (as Miller put it).[30] This centred, holistic methodology had origins, distant as well as proximate, in varied currents of thought: in nineteenth-century romantic philosophy or Alfred North Whitehead's relational 'process' philosophy, which held enormous influence in American letters during the 1930s. The quest for 'centred' understandings of social phenomena, moreover, often had moral or political implications as well, particularly as a critical response to what many critics regarded as the corrosive individualism of modern capitalism and American business ideology in particular.[31] In any case, both common consciousness and academic method held to such holistic deep assumptions just as, fortuitously, power politics set the US 'at the center' of world affairs (as authors of the report NSC-68, the cardinal expression of Cold War in 1950, put it), and new demands for mobilization and morale raised the stakes for definitions of national identity and belonging.[32]

Politics assumed a new cast as American government at mid-century came to bear the traits of a warfare/welfare state. Prodigious centralizing forces directed attention ever more so towards national policymaking and decision, whether those concerned recent innovations in guaranteeing social security to a wide, national public or the towering apparatus of military, diplomatic and intelligence operations. Anticommunism set in as the watchword of both foreign and domestic policy and swiftly narrowed the room for left-wing dissent after the labour struggles of 1945–47 had spurred a brief post-war surge in radicalism. Communist Party activists, having thrown themselves into the Henry Wallace campaign with initial hopes of consolidating a third-party presence in American politics, were thrown back on the defensive as they continued to denounce the Cold War policy that was consolidated as a major-party consensus by 1948–1949 and as espionage trials tarred them as an internal enemy. While Communists had been the largest, most vigorous contingent on the far left, other radicals with anti-Stalinist credentials either suffered stigmatization as well or, under the pressure of events, drifted towards embracing or conceding to the anti-communist mainstream. Aside from the gross distortions of official anti-communist propaganda (particularly, the false claims regarding Soviet aggression towards Greece or Turkey), clear evidence of Stalin's tyranny in Soviet prison camps and in Eastern Europe's repressive regimes drove many American radicals to the right. All left-wing parties lost members, and ardent attempts to sustain an 'independent radicalism' dedicated to supporting 'neither Washington nor Moscow' faltered by 1950.[33]

In intellectual life, the most renowned episode marking the 'de-radicalization' of left-wing writers came in 1952, when the pre-eminent independent literary review, *Partisan Review* (*PR*), convened a symposium entitled 'Our Country and Our Culture,' based on a call for writers to contemplate the strikingly more friendly disposition of modernist intellectuals towards American culture and American democracy than they had avowed 5, 10, or 15 years earlier. Having originated in 1933 as the organ of New York's John Reed Club of Communist-aligned writers, *PR* broke away in the late 1930s to become a venue for anti-Stalinist leftists and modernists resistant to all conformity – including that nationalist spirit signalled by the Communist Party's Popular Front strategy (and the associated celebration of a left-wing Americanism) starting in 1935.[34] For *PR* writers, the note in 1952 of national *belonging* indicated by the first-person plural possessive, 'our,' indeed suggested a turnabout. *PR*'s left-wing anti-Stalinism had already morphed, for many of its contributors, to a more mainstream anti-communism, but the old grudges survived. In late 1948, *PR* denounced Matthiessen bitterly as a 'sentimental fellow-traveler' whose book *From the Heart of Europe* – driven as it was by a Wallace-ite dedication to averting a new war breaking out from East-West tensions – shamelessly whitewashed Soviet tyranny and the perfidy, in particular, of Czech Communists on the eve of their coup in early 1948.[35] Now the author of that assault on Matthiessen, Irving Howe (still self-consciously a member of the radical left), was one of the few dissenters in 'Our Country and Our Culture' to challenge what he saw as the journal's concession to the new conformist patriotism.[36] In an age of cultural nation-building and a publishing rush of new studies diagnosing American character and American civilization, *PR* had apparently joined the fold.

Americanness as a moving target

The impression, however, that a firm nationalistic consensus had gripped intellectual life, wholesale, significantly misreads the mid-century literature on American culture. In fact, the entire enterprise of defining the nature of American identity and culture stumbled on the peculiar stresses of that time, for the attempt to seize on the essence of Americanism lay in torsion with an ongoing transition in American life whose direction was as yet uncertain. The best writers on the question recognized that American character and culture was a moving target, especially so at that moment of substantial change in the order of things; they even hinted that the effort to settle on a definition and description of Americanness was nearly an impossible task.

The most zealous guardians of Americanism, the principal spokesmen of the House Committee on Un-American Activities (HUAC), stood as exemplars of an old America already fading from view (which of course did not mean that they lacked power). Indeed, the very meaning of 'un-American' – that is, the antithesis of whatever it was Progressive-era advocates of 'Americanization' thought they would fashion out of an assimilated mass of immigrants – was uncertain and changing. In its first incarnation as a temporary committee started in 1934 by the Jewish New York congressman Samuel Dickstein, HUAC aimed its fire against pro-German, pro-Nazi propaganda within the US following Hitler's rise to power, antithetical, that is, to Dickstein's identification of American principles with melting-pot tolerance. Dickstein's Special Committee was overtaken in 1938 by a revamped HUAC led by Texas conservative Martin Dies as part of the Southern Democratic backlash against the New Deal. In this right-wing ideological framing, HUAC was turned into a 'permanent' committee of the House in 1945, at the initiative of Mississippi congressman John E. Rankin. Back in the mid-1930s, Rep. Dickstein would have judged the Ku Klux Klan 'un-American' for its intolerance, but in 1946 Rankin summarily dismissed the suggestion that HUAC investigate the Klan: 'After all, the KKK is an old American institution.'[37] Rankin's nation had a colour ('white man's country'), a racial designation that was seconded, in somewhat old-fashioned language, by Texas Rep. Hatton W. Summers, who hailed the Committee for its work in preserving 'the Anglo-Saxon form of government.'[38] Rankin imagined he had scored points against film actors who defended the Hollywood Ten when he revealed their Jewish birth-names: Danny Kaye was really Kaminsky, Edward G. Robinson really Emmanuel Goldenberg, and so forth. But that kind of Americanism was already a relic. Even in the conservative reaches of the US military command, the tradition of regarding the US as a 'Protestant nation' had been cast aside; as wartime

IDEOLOGIES IN ACTION 79

campaigns welcoming Jews and Catholics in the ranks into a 'tri-faith America,' in historian Kevin Schultz's phrase, became 'standard operating procedure.'[39]

Most sophisticated observers at the time believed that the rapid succession of Depression, New Deal, and world war had shifted the country and its way of life onto new ground, a new order of things that they either attempted to descry – or regarded virtually as *terra incognita*. The old order of 'American individualism' and 'rugged' self-reliance receded before a new age of large organizations and government provision of services based on the new-found watchword of 'security,' and most analysts regarded this ongoing transition as salutary. As the most recognizable sociologist of the time (pictured on the cover of *Time* magazine), David Riesman offered a view of the sea-change in American lifeways that has long been misinterpreted as a broadside against mass-society conformism. Although he worried about conformist pressures, Riesman was in fact no hand-wringing Jeremiah. His fundamental argument, posed in terms of character-and-culture studies promoted by the Boasians since the 1930s, was that Americans had once hewed to a model of the 'inner-directed' individual, the classic, 'driven,' self-reliant suitor of success on one's own terms, governed by moral strictures (disciplined work and resistance to temptation) that acted as 'gyroscope' within the self. Now, he claimed, the trend was the emergence of an 'other-directed type,' people not so much driven by a hard core of willpower within but instead guided through life by their attentiveness to the thoughts, feelings, wishes, sentiments of those around them. If the 'gyroscope' had been replaced, in Riesman's clever post-war usage, by 'radar,' the implication might be drawn that Americans were now inclined to follow the herd rather than strike out each on his own. And Riesman had no doubt that 'other direction' in the worst sense could lead to just that, amid all the new forms of large-scale organization and mass media communications that dominated everyday affairs. But because Riesman was sufficiently shaped by the critique of bourgeois society posed during the 1930s and 1940s, he took his distance from the 'Protestant ethic' of disciplined work, moralist independence, and competitive success drives; he refused to mourn the inner-directed man too much. He hoped instead that the other-directed individual would create a more 'socialized' life while nurturing creativity and 'autonomy' at the same time.[40]

Riesman's work demonstrated at least this: once there was a consensus on *attempting* to define 'the American way,' Americans in fact encountered a profoundly *new* American culture. In many respects, the hunters of 'un-American' heresy were painfully obsolete, rooted in an old way of life, declaring forever the greatness of the American entrepreneur, the hardy individualist and Protestant moralizer. Painfully so, we might say, because those defenders of a bygone way could nonetheless wreak great havoc in people's lives and, indeed, contribute to 'other-direction' of the worst (conformist) sort – insofar, that is, as the citizen would 'read the radar' to avoid doing anything the crusading Americanizers considered out of line. This consequence of the Red Scare mentality provides part of the reason that Riesman in the early 1950s – an anti-communist liberal who nonetheless held to a few idiosyncratic radical and pacifist views – repeatedly voiced his discomfort with excessive talk of 'togetherness': not because he longed for the return of the inner-directed standard but because the red hunters might stampede Americans into the self-absorbed family, where they dropped out of the public world of politics, as

Riesman's mentor, Alexis de Tocqueville, warned by pointing out the privatizing streak in American culture.

It was this notion of a sea-change in American society, culture, and personality – changes, however, with uncertain outcomes – that lay at the heart of the varied diagnoses offered by so-called 'consensus historians.' Failure to register this grounding of the 'consensus' writers leads to the misguided interpretation of their work as part of the 'great American celebration,' complicit in efforts to foster national homogeneity, when they actually ventured a fairly sharp cultural criticism of the American past. To be sure, one of the putative 'consensus' historians, Daniel Boorstin, promoted a kind of American exceptionalism in his *Genius of American Politics* – his view of salutary, consensual political traditions that inoculated Americans against the disruptive, extreme ideologies of the Old World – that harked back to the rhetoric of nineteenth-century American pundits recoiling from the European revolutions of 1848.[41] Aside from Boorstin, however, other practitioners of the 'consensus' method in history had quite other aims: rather, they engaged in what I call the disenchantment of America as they examined precisely the flux in American ideologies that the red-hunting vigilance committees of old-line Americanism had tried to arrest. 'Consensus' historiography was in fact a mode of criticism by analysts who hoped to demystify American life, to scatter its illusions.[42]

Let us take three exemplars: Louis Hartz, Richard Hofstadter and F. O. Matthiessen's student Leo Marx. They had emerged from left-wing milieus of the 1930s. By the 1950s, they found themselves, to varying degrees, disenchanted with their own past hopes for radical change, yet they retained enough of their early critical views to recognize and welcome what a later historian called 'the unraveling of America's sacred history.'[43] Hartz famously diagnosed an American heritage built upon the 'liberalism' of John Locke, but it was a heritage not to be glorified; he aimed, instead, 'to drive a wedge of rationality through the pathetic indecisions of social thought,' to reveal the costs of a Lockian mentality that insistently evaded the real conflicts and quandaries that modern social life posed *throughout* the modern world, including the US. Hofstadter was the anatomist of American 'reform,' appearing in different guises such as Populism or Progressivism but commonly disabled by throwbacks to a mythic individualism rooted in yeoman pride or Christian moralism. Marx, followed his teacher Matthiessen in diagnosing antebellum America, and found there a streak of romanticism, a 'pastoral' image of America perfectly balanced between rude nature and social refinement that Melville above all had recognized for what it was – an escapist reverie blind to the brutalities of emerging industrial capitalism. These were the prior modes of consensus, the dominating mentality, of which America was nearly freed as the transforming experience of Depression and war scattered romantic, moralistic, narrow-minded, exceptionalist and self-satisfying illusions. Now the country and its people might acknowledge that they belonged to the world at large rather than standing apart from it; that individuals could not solve all social problems by pursuing private self-interest or upholding inherited standards of moral righteousness; and that in a technologically altered world, things could not be left to set themselves aright but instead required foresight, even planning, to satisfy common needs and expectations. Perhaps, these 'consensus' historians thought, the country was ready to enter modern times on the basis of principles (including some kind of rational collective action) that were quite different from the backward agrarian and commercial individualism that had long-stunted American government, political thought and social policy. Yet, Hartz, Hofstadter and Marx made clear they could not be certain whether Americans would face this challenge or flee from it.[44]

In other words, the enterprise of isolating 'American' traits at mid-century, while fostered by a 50-year run of cultural nation-building and assorted motives for adopting holistic methods, often recognized significant change in the constitution of those traits; the practitioners at some level registered the torsion between a moving reality and efforts to capture it in descriptive terms. 'America,' 'American society' in contrast to Russian society or Japanese society, 'American literature,' etc.: each was something alright – but *what* it was remained a fleeting, fugitive thing. Those venturing to assay Americanness approached the task from any number of perspectives, from Daniel Boorstin's anticommunism to Max Lerner's liberal two volumes, *America as a Civilization* and C. L. R. James's Hegelian Marxist (and Tocquevillian!) account, *American Civilization*, written as he awaited deportation for un-American activities. As a dialectician keenly attuned to flux, James defined American civilization in his time as something new and largely unrecognized, for it was yet taking shape in the popular arts that expressed the insurgency of mass democratic distrust of bourgeois order.[45] Others too sensed that the thing to be defined as distinctively 'American' could hardly be named.

A close reading of the *Partisan Review* symposium, 'Our Country and Our Culture,' reveals this conundrum nicely.[46] Over three numbers of the journal running through the year 1952, a total of 24 prominent writers and critics filled nearly 120 printed pages with reflections on what they would make of the new, post-war mood of acceptance of and belonging within American culture. It was a striking feature of its time that of those 24, no writers of colour appeared in the symposium – and only one woman, Louise Bogan, who by that time had been poetry editor of the *New Yorker* for decades. Nonetheless, the symposium elicited a wide range of opinions, and among the two dozen writers who contributed, sensibilities varied between self-confessed 'despair' about the state of the culture (i.e. for those few who were most distressed by the weight of 'mass culture') and an insistent optimism regarding improving material conditions and prospects. Above all, the most common theme was the de-provincializing of American culture: as poet (and former *New Masses* editor) Horace Gregory put it, for the artist and writer, 'The center of whatever world he can conceive of – for the time being at least – is the US, and Europe is its museum.'[47] More than a relocation of cultural resources from a war-devastated Europe to these shores, de-provincializing implied a move beyond what had struck the observers of decades past as the 'raw' or 'thin' quality of American culture to a new condition in which learning and art-appreciation now really counted; indeed, most agreed that the philistinism once mocked by H. L. Mencken no longer reigned.

Lionel Trilling, in particular, averred that 'art and thought are more generally and happily received and recognized – if not wholly loved – than they have ever been in America,' in part as a result of growing prosperity, communications media, universities that all fostered a 'newly expanded intellectual class,' a 'large intellectual elite' that he welcomed. Moreover, this literary scholar who affirmed the principle, 'Art ... really is the criticism of life' – one who usually stands as a representative of high modernism – saw a democratic thrust to 'the increased power of mind in the nation,' insofar as 'the intellectual and quasi-intellectual classes of contemporary American characteristically push up from the bottom,' exercising a force such that 'mass culture ... might become a better thing than it now is, that it might attract genius.'[48] His point was not smug; mainly he, like David Riesman, insisted that 'America' was something that was undergoing significant change, becoming something quite different than it had been.

A fair number of dissenters within the symposium professed no such optimism; yet almost no one doubted that they could draw judgments, generally, about 'America' and 'American culture.' Only Irving Howe firmly resisted the holistic premise: 'Need we really lose ourselves in such immensities as "America"? Must one hate or love such a grab-bag of abstractions as "America"? ... When the *PR* editors report that writers now "want very much to be part of American life," I cannot react with enthusiasm or distaste until I am told *which part* of American life.'[49] David Riesman too, despite his friendly view of American cultural progress, warned against homogenizing notions of 'Americanization.'

Nonetheless, there was a kind of *negative* uniformity to the contributions, in terms of what was not said. No one even mentioned 'our Negro population' until Max Lerner did at 100 pages into the symposium; no one mentioned the ongoing Korean war despite a rate of some 45 US soldiers dead per day. Only the few most vigorous radicals spoke more generally about the US 'war economy,' and novelist Norman Mailer, then under the influence of an idiosyncratic French Marxist, Jean Malaquais, noted that 'that total war and the total war economy predicate[s] a total regimentation of thought' – though, he noted, the waning of the old, philistine censorship meant that the country, in his view, was now subject to a new kind of stealth repression.[50] C. Wright Mills declined to reflect on intellectuals' proclivity either to 'alienation' from or 'acceptance' of 'our country' – in part because he claimed to adhere to a cultural internationalism (which he named 'the West'). He argued the main problem of his time was the disappearance of a 'movement or party having a chance to influence the course of affairs' in the direction of real change; Howe concurred that socialist movements had died, even though world capitalism, in his view, was still doomed.[51]

Nothing welded the contributors together quite so much as their common endorsement, more or less vehement, of the anti-Soviet role of the US in the world. Even Howe confessed that he no longer 'settle[d] on an isle of rectitude equidistant from both sides' (577); perhaps Mailer and Mills were the only ones to withhold assent to this stance. Otherwise, even as quite a few decried the 'restrictive' atmosphere of the red scare, the bulk of participants ventured some notion that the country had, for good or ill, 'grown up,' 'matured,' reached a kind of 'equilibrium,' achieved a new density of social and cultural institutions, entered upon an 'interregnum' between something achieved and something else yet to come. Surprisingly, given the 'reaffirmation' of American belonging that most contributors avowed and new aesthetic movements (like abstract expressionism) that would later in retrospect be acknowledged as great achievements, quite a few contributors nonetheless claimed their moment was marked by 'stasis,' a lack of 'fresh creative activity' (as Louise Bogan put it), a slack character to American arts.[52]

Moreover, these critics' 'affirmation' of belonging did not, for the most part, lead the writers to identify definite traits that gave 'America' its distinct character. Even Philip Rahv, one of the symposium's conveners and clearly a proponent of taking the American side in the Cold War, confessed discomfort at the revival of the 'illusion that our society is in its very nature immune to tragic social conflicts and collisions' other countries faced. As in Delmore Schwartz's diagnosis of American culture's slack interregnum, Louis Kronenberg remarked that while intellectuals felt 'well-disposed toward America,' they still lacked 'an actual attitude' towards it, which 'in the absence of any driving conviction or emotion, may not even be emerging.' If America and its culture were indeed now at the 'centre' of things, it remained a peculiarly empty centre. As Rahv remarked, 'The rout of the left-wing movement has depoliticized literature – which is not necessarily a bad thing in itself if the political motive had been not simply abandoned but creatively displaced by a root-idea of a different order. No such idea having emerged so far, what is to be observed now is a kind of detachment from principle and fragmentation of the literary life.'[53] His one-time partner, Mary McCarthy, writing for *PR* amid the beginning of Tennessee Williams's career and what is now recognized as the heyday of American musical theatre, claimed that 'the stage presents such a spectacle of confusion, disintegration and despair that no generalization can cover the case.'[54] Oddly, in that time of centring and apparent consolidation, someone saw fragmentation instead.

As far as Rahv was concerned, America and Americanism were no 'root-idea' capable of granting energy to creative writing once dedication to sharp social and political criticism had been surrendered. America and Americanism remained words to denote something, something defined largely by what it was not (the foreign enemy) – about which the urge to say *something* was compelling, but which eluded a meaningful definition still. The meaning of America, Americanism, American culture or American character might be regarded as something like Sigmund Freud's trouble in defining his 'Jewish' identity: If in light of his irreligion, ignorance of Hebrew, and antipathy to nationalism you were to ask him, Freud wrote in the third person, 'What is Jewish about you, when you have given up all these common characteristics with your people? he would answer, a great deal still, probably the most important thing of all. But he would not be able to express this essential thing in clear words.'[55] Gerald Izenberg has argued that Freud's 'puzzlement' reflected most his 'liberal individualist' principles averse to group identity; we might interpret it, also and otherwise, as a testament to the inability to define the substance or 'content' of such identifiers. That content is fugitive and in that sense absent.

National culture between past and future

Examining what was *absent* from *PR*'s symposium sheds further light on the problem of defining American culture or finding within it a place of belonging. A few months earlier, James Baldwin, as yet only 27 years old, wrote in *PR*, 'The story of the Negro in America is the story of America – or more precisely, it is the story of Americans. It is not a very pretty story.' Baldwin captured all the weirdness of the 'Our Culture' discussion by addressing the 'things unsaid' there, i.e. the story, he now wrote, 'which no American is prepared to hear.'[56] And Baldwin, in this essay entitled, 'Many Thousands Gone' – from the old folk song, 'No More Auction Block,' that African Americans sang to mourn their forebears as they were achieving emancipation – does not *relate* that story so much as allude to it – as unrelatable. The essay talks about Bigger Thomas, the protagonist of Richard Wright's 1941 novel *Native Son*, who never appears to the reader as a knowable person ('we know as little about him when this journey is ended as we did when it began') but rather as the image of 'simple, naked and unanswerable hatred' (for what 'Negro living in America ... has not wanted to smash any white face he may encounter in a day'?), nurtured by the relentless 'dehumanization of the Negro [that] is indivisible from our dehumanization of ourselves.'[57] 'Our dehumanization' here refers to 'we' Americans in the strange diction or voice that Baldwin maintained throughout this essay: 'Americans' always are cited in the first person, 'we' and 'our,' while 'the Negro' figures always in the third person, 'he,' as if Baldwin himself is 'American' and *not* black. These are the signals of that the irresolvable strangeness, of belonging and not belonging, that Baldwin ascribed to African Americans: *of* but not *in* the country, because they are both excluded and yet the same as the country itself, constituting the only 'true story' to tell about America. Baldwin, throughout his early essays, constantly recognizes 'schisms in the mind' that reflect such coincident opposites.[58] In his view, Wright had failed 'to convey any sense of Negro life as a continuing and complex group reality' just as Bigger remains 'blank'; but rather than indicating a failure by the novelist, this tells of the novel's verisimilitude, for the nation's 'identity' remains blank, 'annulled,' so long as the real violence and oppression of the American past is denied by myths of the free and the brave.[59]

Baldwin played upon such paradoxes, recognizing in Wright's title, 'Native Son,' all the ambiguities of American identity and culture, for Bigger was a 'native son' as was Baldwin himself. In his 1955 essay, 'Notes of a Native Son,' Baldwin remembered the simultaneity of his father's death and the Harlem riot of 1943. 'The Negro in America,' he wrote, is 'native' to a culture that utterly denies his humanity, indeed his reality. And by, thus, making 'the Negro' unknowable, just as Bigger is unknowable to himself, the country establishes its single most definitive trait – its 'innocence' (or denial) and hence its constitutive inauthenticity. Baldwin offered his own definition of national culture, of 'American' traits, as he identified an 'American psychology' whose inclination to denial made it impossible to acknowledge and understand 'the darkness which lies behind' until that mentality 'undergo[es] a metamorphosis so profound as to be literally unthinkable and which there is no doubt we will resist until we are compelled to achieve our own identity by the rigors of a time that has yet to come.'[60] Baldwin's Americanism was something not existent but yet to be 'achieved.' In his meditation on his father's funeral, remembering a man who was almost thoroughly bitter and cruel, Baldwin ended with the self-demand to 'hold in mind forever two ideas which seemed to be in opposition': 'acceptance, totally without rancor, of life as it is' combined with the need nonetheless to fight the injustices of that existence resolutely, with a 'heart free of hatred and despair.' That is when this native son, knowing his 'father was irrecoverable ... wished that he had been beside me so that I could have searched his face for the answers which only the future would give me now.'[61]

Here, allusion to a truth that can never be recovered from the past but must be constructed – a future project – echoes an intriguing note in Matthiessen's *American Renaissance*. Matthiessen clearly wrote about the 'Renaissance' period, as his student Leo Marx did in *Machine in the Garden*, as one that first forecast the course of capitalist development and the inescapable need of a more socialized existence. Back then, in the early dawning of industrialism, Matthiessen saw the immature signs of 'our newer mutual dependence,' or the social interdependence of modernity that was, in his own time, more evident and yet still insufficiently realized. His Christian socialism showed through; indeed, he saw his time as a pregnant one just as the 1840s were. And hence his constant return to 'possibilities,' to unrecognized 'opportunities,' the 'unexpressed abundance' of American life, and to Emerson's dictum that 'it is the faculty of the poet to see present things as if ... also past and future.' Thus, while 'Melville could feel that the deepest need for rapaciously individualist America was a radical affirmation of the heart,' it was Whitman who was best able to make that affirmation, and hence serve (partly) as the Hegelian synthesis of the light and dark biases of the previous four writers in Matthiessen's treatment. For Whitman believed insistently in 'the fresh opportunities for the English tongue' in the 'whole range of American facts,' and his ability to 'release "new potentialities" of expression for our native character.' There is something Joycean in Matthiessen's depiction of Whitman, a devotion like Stephen Daedalus to 'forge the *uncreated* consciousness' of the country and its 'previously unexpressed' abundance. For Matthiessen, this project was less a matter of pinpointing the substance of 'America' in its past; rather he suggested, as in a passage of Nietzsche he quoted at the end of *American Renaissance*, that only 'the architect of the future can hope to decipher' the meanings presented to us by the past. Even Matthiessen, in probing 'American characteristics' in literature, suggested that 'America' did not exist but was yet to be, something not to know but yet to be achieved. He shared 'the belief in *the possibility of a* native culture' rather than faith in its presence or its preservation.[62]

Let us then return to Baldwin and his remarkable essays of 1962–63, joined in the book *The Fire Next Time*, which clearly built on his 1952 perspective in 'Many Thousands Gone' but also appeared at a time that marked the end of the Fifties moment concerned with the 'centred' definition of Americanness. In these later essays, he declared, bluntly, 'The American Negro has the great advantage of having never believed the collection of myths to which white Americans cling: that their ancestors were all freedom-loving heroes, that they were born in the greatest country the world has ever seen, or that Americans are invincible in battle and wise in peace ...'[63] It was a bracing declaration, a bit gentler than Malcolm X's designation of Negroes as 'victims of Americanism' and perhaps by now, as historians focus ever greater attention on the nationally constitutive role of slavery and white supremacy, almost a commonplace. Yet, Baldwin's idea remains challenging to plumb and to fully inhabit. When so many writers at mid-century contemplated 'the very question of America and its meaning,' Baldwin's *The Fire Next Time* upended the whole debate.[64] He was no Black nationalist and, notwithstanding his expatriate life in France, no 'emigrationist,' for he believed that blacks in the US were, socially and culturally, wholly *of* if not *in* (in the integrationist sense) this country; and yet, given the deep corruption in the national past, there was no 'meaning' to return to, to reclaim, realize or vindicate as a promise of black freedom. Again, the verb Baldwin chose, in a determinedly existentialist vein, was to '*achieve* our country' – to create a viable moral meaning for national identity where none as yet existed.[65] It was yet to come, if at all.

The best writers on American culture in the mid-twentieth century recognized the elusive quality of what they sought to define and describe. What shall we call the *ideology* of 'Americanism': the faulty effort to freeze a moment and identify its meaning with some inevitably loaded vision of a past heritage – or, on the other hand, the varied,

86   IDEOLOGIES IN ACTION

sophisticated inquiries into the nation's complex, unsynthesized history and the uncertain, potential futures it has made possible?

Notes

1. 'Our Country and Our Culture, II', *Partisan Review*, 19 (1952), p. 426.
2. S. Bellow, *The Adventures of Augie March* (New York: Fawcett, 1965), p. 557.
3. *Mon Oncle d'Amerique*, directed by Alain Resnais (New York: New Yorker Video, 2000), DVD.
4. F. O. Matthiessen, *American Renaissance: Art and Expression in the Age of Emerson and Whitman* (1941; New York: Barnes & Noble, 2009), p. xii.
5. Matthiessen, ibid., p. xii-xiii.
6. Matthiessen, *ibid.*, xv, xix, pp. 685–717.
7. Matthiessen, ibid., p. 713.
8. Matthiessen, ibid., p. xxi.
9. Matthiessen, ibid., pp. 81, 181, 189, 191, 134, 144.
10. H. N. Smith, 'The Salzburg Seminar', *American Quarterly*, 1 (1949), pp. 30–37.
11. F.O. Matthiessen, *From the Heart of Europe* (New York: Oxford University Press, 1948), p. 1.
12. Quoted in John Rackliffe, 'Notes for a Character Study', *Monthly Review*, 2 (1950), pp. 259–260.
13. For a related critique of historicism, see Dipesh Chakrabarty, *Provincializing Europe Postcolonial Thought and Historical Difference* (Princeton, NJ: Princeton University Press, 2000).
14. The dismissal with American Studies of holistic vision of culture was already evident in the 1980s. An attempt to resist that trend and reanimate holistic analyses is H. Varenne (Ed), *Symbolizing America* (Lincoln : University of Nebraska Press, 1986).
15. W. Wall, *Inventing the 'American Way': The Politics of Consensus from the New Deal to the Civil Rights Movement* (New York: Oxford University Press, 2008).
16. J. Butler, *Becoming America: The Revolution before 1776* (Cambridge, MA: Harvard University Press, 2000).
17. H. D. Croly, *The Promise of American Life* (New York: The Macmillan Company, 1914).
18. M. Green, *New York 1913: The Armory Show and the Paterson Strike Pageant* (New York: Scribner, 1988); V. W. Brooks, *America's Coming-of-Age* (New York: B. W. Huebsch, 1915); C. N. Blake, *Beloved Community: The Cultural Criticism of Randolph Bourne, van Wyck Brooks, Waldo Frank, and Lewis Mumford* (Chapel Hill, NC: University of North Carolina Press, 1990); D. H. Borus, *Twentieth-Century Multiplicity: American Thought and Culture, 1900–1920* (Lanham, MD: Rowman & Littlefield, 2009).
19. J. T. Sparrow, *Warfare State: World War II Americans and the Age of Big Government* (New York: Oxford University Press, 2011); G. Lipsitz, *Rainbow at Midnight: Labor and Culture in the 1940s* (Urbana, IL: University of Illinois Press, 1994); N. Lichtenstein, *A Contest of Ideas: Capital, Politics, and Labor* (Urbana, IL: University of Illinois Press, 2013).
20. P. V. Murphy, *The New Era: American Thought and Culture in the 1920s* (Lanham, MD: Rowman & Littlefield, 2012); K. M. Schultz, *Tri-Faith America: How Catholics and Jews Held Postwar America to Its Protestant Promise* (New York: Oxford University Press, 2011); D. A. Hollinger, *After Cloven Tongues of Fire: Protestant Liberalism in Modern American History* (Princeton, NJ: Princeton University Press, 2013).
21. On the Melville revival, see F. G. Robinson, *Love's Story Told: A Life of Henry A. Murray* (Cambridge, MA: Harvard University Press, 1992). On the study of American literature, L. Maddox, *Locating American Studies: The Evolution of a Discipline* (Baltimore, MA: Johns Hopkins University Press, 1999), p. 177, n. 15.
22. J. B. Hubbell, 'Foreword', *American Literature*, 1 (1929), p. 2.
23. B. Blower, *Becoming Americans in Paris: Transatlantic Politics and Culture between the World Wars* (Oxford: New York: Oxford University Press, 2011).

24. H. Stearns, *America; a Re-Appraisal* (New York: Hillman-Curl, 1937).
25. P. Miller, *Errand into the Wilderness* (Cambridge: Belknap Press of Harvard University Press, 1956); G. Wise, '"Paradigm Dramas" in American Studies: A Cultural and Institutional History of the Movement', in Maddox, *Locating American Studies, op. cit.*, Ref. 21, pp. 174–176.
26. A. Kazin, *On Native Grounds: An Interpretation of Modern American Prose Literature*, 3rd Harvest ed. (New York: Harcourt, Brace and Company, 1995).
27. Matthiessen, *From the Heart of Europe, op. cit.*, Ref. 11, p. 31; R. M. Cook, *Alfred Kazin: A Biography* (New Haven: Yale University Press, 2007), pp. 120–123.
28. Miller, quoted by Wise, in Maddox, *Locating American Studies, op. cit.*, Ref. 21, pp. 175–176 (emphasis added).
29. R. Williams, *Culture and Society, 1780–1950* (London: Chatto & Windus, 1958); H. Brick, *Transcending Capitalism: Visions of a New Society in Modern American Thought* (Ithaca: Cornell University Press, 2006), pp. 86–98.
30. Brick, *Transcending Capitalism, ibid.*, pp. 121–151.
31. Brick, ibid., pp. 98–120; H. Brick, 'Discipline, Craft and Culture: The Politics of Holistic Thought', *Michigan Quarterly Review*, 31 (1992), pp. 128–142.
32. E. R. May and National Security Council (U.S.), *American Cold War Strategy: Interpreting NSC 68* (Boston: Bedford Books of St. Martin's Press, 1993), p. 54.
33. G. D. Sumner, *Dwight MacDonald and the Politics Circle* (Ithaca: Cornell University Press, 1996); H. Brick and C. Phelps, *Radicals in America: The U.S. Left since the Second World War* (New York: Cambridge University Press, 2015), pp. 41–48.
34. On the reinvention of *Partisan Review* after 1936 and its critique of Popular Front Americanism, see A. M. Wald, *The New York Intellectuals: The Rise and Decline of the Anti-Stalinist Left from the 1930s to the 1980s*, Thirtieth Anniversary Edition (Chapel Hill, NC: University of North Carolina Press, 2017), pp. 80–97. For a favourable view from the left of Popular Front Americanism, see M. Denning, *The Cultural Front: The Laboring of American Culture in the Twentieth Century* (London: Verso, 1996), especially pp. 130–135, and M. Denning, '"The Special American Conditions": Marxism and American Studies,' *American Quarterly*, 38:3 (1986): 356–380. Wald points out the close connection between *Partisan Review*'s critiques of Popular Front Americanism and of 'mass culture'; the latter animus clearly continued in the *PR* milieu long after the demise of the Communists' Popular Front period of the 1930s. See *The New York Intellectuals*, p. 223.
35. I. Howe, 'The Sentimental Fellow-Traveling of F. O. Matthiessen', *Partisan Review*, 15 (1948), pp. 1125–1129.
36. I. Howe, in 'Our Country and Our Culture,' *Partisan Review* 19 (1952), pp. 575–581.
37. M. Newton, *The Ku Klux Klan in Mississippi: a History* (Jefferson, NC: McFarland & Co., 2010), p. 102.
38. W. Goodman, *The Committee; the Extraordinary Career of the House Committee on Un-American Activities.* (New York: Farrar, Straus, and Giroux, 1968), p. 183.
39. Schultz, *Tri-Faith America, op cit.*, Ref. 20.
40. D. Riesman, *The Lonely Crowd: A Study of the Changing American Character* (New Haven: Yale University Press, 1950); Brick, *Transcending Capitalism, op. cit.*, Ref. 29, pp.172–180.
41. D. J. Boorstin, *The Genius of American Politics* (Chicago: University of Chicago Press, 1953); T. M. Roberts, *Distant Revolutions: 1848 and the Challenge to American Exceptionalism* (Charlottesville: University of Virginia Press, 2009).
42. H. Brick, 'The Disenchantment of America: Radical Echoes in 1950s Political Criticism', in Kathleen G. Donohue (Ed), *Liberty and Justice for All?: Rethinking Politics in Cold War America* (Amherst: University of Massachusetts Press, 2012).
43. M. B. Young, 'The Age of Global Power', in Thomas Bender (Ed) *Rethinking American History in a Global Age* (Berkeley, CA: University of California Press, 2002), p. 288.
44. L. Hartz, *The Liberal Tradition in America; an Interpretation of American Political Thought since the Revolution* (New York: Harcourt, Brace, 1955); R. Hofstadter, *The Age of Reform:*

From Bryan to F.D.R. (New York: Vintage Books, 1955); L. Marx, *The Machine in the Garden; Technology and the Pastoral Ideal in America* (New York: Oxford University Press, 1964).

45. M. Lerner, *America as a Civilization; Life and Thought in the United States Today* (New York: Simon and Schuster, 1957); C. L. R. James, *American Civilization*, (Cambridge, MA: Blackwell, 1993).

46. 'Our Country and Our Culture', *Partisan Review*, 19 (1942), pp. 282–326, 420–450, 562–597.

47. 'Our Country and Our Culture, II', *Partisan Review*, 19 (1952), p. 438.

48. 'Our Country and Our Culture', *Partisan Review*, 19 (1952), pp. 321–322.

49. 'Our Country and Our Culture, III', *Partisan Review*, 19 (1952), p. 580.

50. 'Our Country and Our Culture, I', *op. cit.*, p. 100.

51. 'Our Country and Our Culture, II', *op. cit.*, pp. 446–450.

52. 'Our Country and Our Culture, III', *op. cit.*, pp. 562–565, 577.

53. 'Our Country and Our Culture, III', *ibid.*, pp. 307–309; 'Our Country and Our Culture, II', *op. cit.*, pp. 440–441.

54. D. Reid, *The Brazen Age: New York City and the American Empire: Politics, Art, and Bohemia* (New York: Pantheon Books, 2016), p. 44.

55. Freud, quoted in G. Izenberg, *Identity: The Necessity of a Modern Idea* (University of Pennsylvania Press, 2016), p. 14.

56. J. Baldwin, 'Many Thousands Gone', *Partisan Review* 18 (1951), reprinted in Baldwin, *Notes of a Native Son* (Boston: Beacon Press, 1957), p. 24.

57. Baldwin, *ibid.*, pp. 35, 38, 25.

58. Baldwin, 'Notes of a Native Son', *Harper's*, November 1955, reprinted in Baldwin, *ibid.*, p. 106.

59. Baldwin, *ibid.*, p. 39.

60. Baldwin, *ibid.*, p. 36.

61. Baldwin, *ibid.*, pp. 113–114.

62. Matthiessen, *American Renaissance, op. cit.*, Ref. 4, pp. 372, 712, 559, 563–564, 378, emphasis added.

63. J. Baldwin, *The Fire Next Time* (New York: Dell, 1963), p. 136.

64. A. Hartman, *A War for the Soul of America: A History of the Culture Wars* (Chicago: University of Chicago Press, 2015), p. 10.

65. Baldwin, *Fire Next Time, op cit.*, Ref. 63, p. 141, emphasis added.

Disclosure statement

No potential conflict of interest was reported by the authors.

Democratic babies? Françoise Dolto, Benjamin Spock and the ideology of post-war parenting advice

Richard Bates

ABSTRACT

This article looks at the political implications of a subject not always thought of as directly political, but which has an important ideological component: child-rearing advice. The period after 1945 offers an important example of how this topic can interact with developments in political ideology. This article takes the example of France, with substantial comparative reference to the US and Britain. It argues that the mid-twentieth century was characterized by a move from a hygienist and behaviourist approach to child rearing to a more liberal, humanist approach informed by Freudian psychoanalysis. This occurred significantly later in France – in the 1970s – than in Britain or the US, where it is associated with the years immediately after World War II. Through a comparison of two celebrated childcare experts who epitomized the change – Françoise Dolto in France, Benjamin Spock in the US – the paper explores the reasons for this temporal discrepancy. It shows that Anglo-American experts believed that the widespread application of psychoanalytic theory would help produce democratic citizens and ward off the dangers of authoritarian personalities. In France, psychoanalytic approaches became allied with conservative Catholic views of the family and women's roles, with implications for family policy into the twenty-first century.

Introduction

Child-rearing advice is not always thought of as directly political, at least by the parents and parents-to-be who seek its authority. Yet, a significant and growing body of historical research has made compelling arguments for the need to look at theories of childhood as highly political. The mid-twentieth-century period, in particular, offers an important example of how trends in childrearing can interact with shifting political ideologies in the context of broader social change.

This article examines the place of psychoanalytic thinking in the shift from a hygienist and behaviourist approach to child rearing to a more liberal, child-centred, humanist approach in the second half of the twentieth century. It will focus in particular on the case of France, but with substantial reference to the US and Britain. It will use a comparison between two prominent icons of parenting advice in their respective cultures – Françoise Dolto, in the French case, and Benjamin Spock for the

US – as a way into understanding this cultural change and its relationship to wider political and ideological fields. It will show that Spock's and Dolto's approaches, intellectual influences and personal backgrounds contain some striking similarities, and that their thinking broadly overlapped with that of influential British paediatricians and educationalists such as Donald Winnicott and Susan Isaacs. The element common to all of these thinkers was the combination of a Freudian understanding of children's psychical development with a child-centred, anti-disciplinarian approach to pedagogy, informed by education theorists such as John Dewey, Maria Montessori, Célestin Freinet, and Friedrich Froebel.

Of the thinkers discussed here, Dolto is by far the least known outside of France. Within France, however, Dolto (1908–1988), a child psychoanalyst and paediatrician, had an enormous impact in shaping attitudes to child rearing and child psychology in the latter part of the twentieth century. Certainly from the mid-1970s to the 1990s, and to a lesser extent into the twenty-first century, Dolto was a household name in France, enjoying a degree of respect bordering on veneration from parts of the French state and populace. Across France, hundreds of public institutions – roads, schools, crèches, children's centres, hospital wings – are named after her.[1] Cultural commentators have referred to a 'Dolto generation' of children brought up on her ideas.[2] Yet Dolto, despite arriving at her ideas at more or less the same time as her Anglo-American counterparts, only became a national celebrity some 30 years after them.

This article will explain and explore this discrepancy in terms of comparative national history. It will show that Dolto and Spock arrived at similar ideas at a similar time: the late 1930s. Thereafter, their trajectories diverged significantly. During and after the World War II, policymakers in Britain and the US were attracted by the apparent potential of psycho-analysis to aid the construction of 'democratic citizens' and ward off the formation of authoritarian personalities. In France, no such clear identification between psychoanalysis and democracy occurred at this time. The relationship between psychoanalysis and family politics in France was influenced by the strength of Catholic discourses on the family and gender roles, which were echoed by some French psychoanalysts, and by the political character of French psychoanalysis in the 1940s. Although, as Sarah Fishman has shown, the ideas of Sigmund Freud, along with those of Alfred Kinsey and Simone de Beauvoir, were a significant influence on French discussions of gender and sexuality in the 1950s, only after the cultural changes of the late 1960s did psychoanalysis become as central in French psychiatry and popular culture as it had been in the US after 1945.[3] Dolto's rise to prominence occurred in that context.

The case of Dolto and of France, therefore, adds a degree of complication to the identification, by Dagmar Herzog, Michal Shapira and others, of the immediate post-war decades as the period 'when psychoanalysis gained the greatest traction, across the West'.[4] In France, I would contend, the peak would be more accurately ascribed to the approximate period of 1965–2000. This suggests that explanations for the success of psychoanalysis cannot assume a uniform effect of the World War II and need to be thoroughly situated in confluences of ideological forces occurring in different places at different times.

This article contends that Dolto's popularity from the 1970s in France occurred in the context of a distinctive combination, on the one hand, of anti-authoritarian and child-centred attitudes to parenting and education, and on the other, somewhat patriarchal attitudes to family and gender roles – with psychoanalysis enlisted in support of both of these stances. It will build on recent work by Herzog, Shapira, Camille Robcis, and Tara Zahra among others to suggest that this combination has strong resonances with that which could be found in the US in the 1940s and specifically in the writings of Spock, but which was waning by the 1970s, just at the point at which it was coming to the fore in France.[5]

Raising the democratic citizen in post-war America and Britain

Benjamin Spock's *The Common Sense Book of Baby and Child Care*, first published in 1946, was the best-known parenting and child-care reference manual for American parents during the baby boom. It outsold everything bar the Bible in the second half of the century; by 1998, it had sold 50 million copies and been translated into 42 languages. Although it is indelibly associated with the post-war decades, historians such as Cathy Urwin and Elaine Sharland have interpreted Spock's work as an intellectual product of the interwar years.[6] In particular, it is seen as a reaction to the impersonal and dogmatic tone of early twentieth-century child-rearing literature.[7] Authors such as Truby King, Luther Emmett Holt and the behaviourist John B. Watson posited that children should be subject to rigid feeding schedules and discouraged from displaying or receiving emotion.[8] Holt contended that the critical thing was to communicate to parents the crucial discoveries of nineteenth-century science regarding hygiene and infection; mothers could not rely on love and instinct, but needed scientific knowledge and hygienic discipline to induce good habits in their children. Watson, enthused by the findings of laboratory-based behavioural psychology, believed that children were essentially blank slates and could be conditioned away from undesirable behaviours. Watson saw as undesirable anything that appeared effeminate or soft, arguing that kissing children was unhygienic and risked somehow 'spoiling' children emotionally.

By the 1930s, some psychoanalytically oriented thinkers were beginning to argue for a different approach, partly as a reaction against the above and partly out of enthusiasm for the possibilities that the new Freudian approach offered. In Britain, much work in this direction had been done in the 1920s and 1930s by female psychoanalysts and psycho-analytically oriented thinkers, especially Melanie Klein, Susan Isaacs, and after 1938, Anna Freud and Dorothy Burlingham. These women argued for the importance of children's self- and social development through imaginative play, and for the principle of treating children as fully human subjects. Isaacs was especially innovative in seeking to combine psychoanalysis with ideas of child-centred education.[9] In 1924, Isaacs and Geoffrey Pyke set-up the Malting House School as a centre for child-centred pedagogy along the lines set out by Montessori and Froebel. It stressed play and active learning, as well as an environment that would seek to use Freudian insights to avoid creating 'trauma and repression' in its pupils.[10]

For these early psychoanalytically informed educationalists, and even more for later psychoanalytic paediatricians like Spock, Winnicott and Bowlby, the problem with hygienist and behaviourist approaches was that they tended to objectify or dehumanize children. Such authors contended that the interwar experts had encouraged an attitude of parental detachment from children, who were discursively treated as a commodity, or as analogous to domesticated animals (Truby King, for example, had sought to cross-apply scientific management techniques from livestock farming). Instead, it was necessary to assert – as in the title of Anderson and Mary Aldrich's 1939 book that epitomized the change in tone – that 'babies are human beings'.[11] At this time, this conceptual leap was harder to make than it may seem in retrospect. Winnicott once remarked that it took him 5 years of practising as a child physician to understand that a baby was human at all.[12] Spock himself based the upbringing of his first child on Holt's directives.[13]

Why was the idea that children were fully, autonomously human, deserving of love and compassion and understanding as important individuals in their own right, hard to accept? While space does not permit a full exploration of this question here, historians of the family such as Antoine Prost, Mathew Thomson and Edward Shorter – as well as Eli Zaretsky's recent work on the political history of psychoanalysis – have suggested that the idea arrived as part of a long-term shift in the social and economic function of the family.[14] These writers describe a move from large, high-mortality families operating primarily as economic units, to nuclear families that also functioned as a source of emotional comfort and leisure. Industrialization, urbanization, decreased infant mortality, improved nutrition, hygiene and medicine all played a role in this change. On this reading, part of the explanation for the twentieth-century spread of psychoanalytic thinking lies in its contribution to changing the function of the family from an economic collective to what Prost calls 'the final refuge of the individual' – a major, fundamental shift, and, thus, one that encountered significant resistance.[15]

This is a useful perspective, but it risks neglecting more contingent social and ideological histories. For example, advances in urban public health and in medicine made the hygienists' message seemed less urgent than it had at the beginning of the century. Psychoanalysis, meanwhile, first became a mass cultural phenomenon in the aftermath of the World War I, in the context of serious questioning both of the value of disciplinarian militaristic education, and of women's roles within the family and in broader society. Its history cannot be considered independently of these factors, which form the basis of my contextualization here.

An essential component of the psychoanalytic approach was childhood determinism: the idea that children's early life experiences would, by shaping the unconscious of the future adult, have a crucial bearing on later character and life chances. Frequently, this was framed negatively, in terms of the damage that a psychologically unhealthy upbringing could cause – perhaps without the parents even being aware of the lasting harm they were facilitating. Isaacs, for example, hoped that psychoanalysis would become the foundation for a scientific understanding of the child's mind, comparable to the 'proved scientific knowledge about food and sleep and clothing' that had improved children's life chances in preceding decades.[16] Without such an understanding, 'we move in the dark, and may do much harm, with the best intentions in the world'.[17] The child's psyche became a privileged site for expert knowledge; psychoanalysis, in this context, appeared to be an important tool for shaping the citizenry of the future. This had political implications. If the early childhood years were crucial, then educating the public in child psychology was vital. At scale, and in the context of expanding welfare provision after 1945, this implied the involvement of the state.

The task of understanding children's psychological and emotional development was rendered all the more urgent by the geopolitical situation. If children were not brought up to be emotionally contented and psychologically stable, might they not be attracted to political extremes? As Gwen St Aubyn's *Family Book* of 1935 put it, 'the neglected

IDEOLOGIES IN ACTION 93

toddler in everyone's way is the material which becomes the disgruntled agitator, while the happy contented child is the pillar of the State'.[18]

In Britain and the US, 1940s public policy was inflected with a perceived need to ensure the production of democratic citizens, in the face of the threat from the 'totalitarian' ideologies of Nazism and Communism. Psychoanalysts offered tools for identifying psychologically disturbed children and treating their incipient pathologies. Shapira has shown how psychoanalytic ideas resonated with judges and civil servants in 1940s Britain.[19] They 'became common parlance for a wider public ... transforming both public policy and the individual experiences of citizens of diverse backgrounds, and advancing new concepts of self and mental health'. The attitudes of social workers and the treatment of criminals – especially 'juvenile delinquents', a source of major concern and enormous discursive output – became substantially influenced by psychoanalysis. Often this was done in the name of protecting democracy. Psychoanalysis, argues Shapira, 'helped produce new expectations for selfhood, citizenship, mental health, and the emergent social democracy'.[20] For Donald Winnicott, who disliked state centralization and opposed Britain's creation of the National Health Service on the grounds that it 'nationalised doctors', humanist psychoanalysis suggested a vision of small-scale institutions run by people, not bureaucracies. Winnicott envisioned psychoanalysis informing parenting in ordinary homes, populated by 'good enough mothers' and producing stable, civic-minded individuals.[21]

Using psychoanalysis to encourage the development of democratic practices in the family was likewise a central strand of Spock's approach. Influenced by the social scientist Lawrence K. Frank, Spock thought that those who followed dictators were driven by repressed anxieties and resentments.[22] *Baby and Child Care* was strongly informed by a Freudian view of the psyche and of child development. Concepts such as the Oedipus complex, castration anxiety and psychosomatic conversion were prominent, though Spock chose not to use Freud's terms. He hoped that the disciplinarian and militaristic overtones of early twentieth-century education would be replaced by a model in which the child was (at least occasionally) a participant in decision-making. Faced with the charge of 'permissiveness' from McCarthy-era conservatives – whose activities are a reminder of the darker side to the American commitment to 'democratic norms' in this period – Spock responded that he was in fact in favour of a different, democratic, kind of discipline. A good school should teach 'democracy, not just as a patriotic motto but as a way of getting things done ... This is the very highest kind of discipline. This training, this spirit, is what makes the best citizens, the most valuable workers ... the finest soldiers'.[23] William Graebner has argued that Spock should be seen as 'nothing less than a social engineer' – that he sought to influence the child-rearing process to 'create a society that was more cooperative, more consensus-oriented, more group-conscious, more knowable, more consistent, and more comforting'.[24]

Spock significantly expanded the range of topics covered by child-rearing manuals beyond practical questions of feeding and hygiene, to engage with psychological anxieties and dilemmas with a social component. As well as the development of good manners, his book counselled parents on their responses to such topics as jealousy, sibling rivalry and sex education. He tried to reassure parents not to be taken in by what would later be termed 'moral panics' over comics, TV and cinema, explaining how things might appear from the child's standpoint, and why children might become confused or traumatized. Rather than prescribed answers, he generally left parents to make up their own minds.

Spock's vision of democratic social engineering through child rearing drew on John Dewey's view of the role of education in creating democratic habits of mind. For Dewey, 'a democracy is more than a form of government; it is primarily a mode of associated living, of conjoint communicated experience'.[25] In *Democracy and Education* (1916), Dewey discussed the concept of 'transmission': the communication of social institutions and practices from one generation to the next by inculcating habits of doing, thinking and feeling.[26] Desirable intellectual and moral habits, such as calm reflection, creative action and consideration of the wider world, were to be transmitted through human interactions; Dewey saw the human individual as a social being from birth. For him, democracy was a way of being and acting, not an idea; a form of associated, communicative living; always a work in progress. To create a democratic society, teachers could not treat children as blank slates or empty vessels into which ideas could be placed; ideas were not like objects. Education should be an interaction between child and curriculum, taking the child's existing desires and imaginative life as a starting point. Teachers needed to engage children in patterns of communication and behaviour that would help develop democratic habits of mind. 'Democratic ends demand democratic methods for their realisation', Dewey wrote.[27]

Dewey's liberal pedagogy was, thus, a good fit with the psychoanalytic emphasis on the importance of child rearing for producing democratic citizens. For Dewey, authoritarian political forms were characterized by a lack of shared communication; universal access to a suitably communicative form of education was, thus, the best way to avoid authoritarianism.[28] Spock was introduced to Dewey's ideas by Caroline B. Zachry at the New York Psychoanalytic Institute in 1934 and saw that they could be extended into the sphere of infant parenting.[29]

As Lisa Farley has shown, Winnicott used his BBC broadcasts not just to argue for, but to model the 'reliable environment' that he thought families should provide for their children.[30] In *Baby and Child Care*, Spock likewise attempted to model or exemplify in microcosm the informed, democratic society he hoped to inhabit. It mattered for Spock that parents and teachers practise what they preach, and embody and enact democratic norms and behaviours. 'A good teacher', he wrote, 'knows that she can't teach democracy out of a book if she's acting like a dictator in person'.[31] Spock hoped parents and children would internalize democratic discipline. A properly led child, he argued, will want to go to bed on time and eat nutritious food without needing to be forced.

A recent article by Shaul Bar-Haim raises the possibility that there was also a sociological dimension to the promotion of liberal and democratic values by pioneering psychoanalysts and educators; that is, the clientele they catered to tended to belong to a professional, artistic or academic elite that espoused those values particularly strongly. Some of the parents of children at Malting House school were central figures in the intellectual community of Cambridge, including Nobel Prize winners and the philosopher G.E. Moore. Bar-Haim argues that Susan Isaacs, a socialist in her youth, was drawn into a 'cultural liberal environment' at Malting House.[32] A similar point might be made in relation to Spock, whose patients in the 1930s and 1940s were largely drawn from highly educated, upper middle-class Manhattan families. Thomas Maier has argued that Spock's reputation was partly down to his ability to assuage the anxieties of the lawyers and artists whose children he saw.[33]

For Spock, his British counterparts, and their clients, democracy would be preserved by maintaining the stability of the family environment and ensuring that families were thoroughly inculcated with democratic values. This, Spock argued, had important consequences for women's place in society. Mothers were expected to provide reliable, reassuring environments for children, with the implication that it would not be desirable for them to work outside the home:

> If a mother realizes clearly how vital this kind of care is to a small child, it may make it easier for her to decide that the extra money she might earn, or the satisfaction she might receive from an outside job, is not so important, after all.[34]

Spock thought that a child growing up in the chaos created by the war and the Great Depression needed unequivocally gendered role models within a heterosexual home.[35] In particular, a boy 'must have the inspiration of a manly father in order to develop his own manliness and courage'.[36] A father could also help his daughter to be feminine by 'complimenting her on her dress, or hair-do, or the cake she's made'.[37] Winnicott similarly saw full-time motherhood as crucial to the democratic national community.[38] In 1939, he warned of the severe 'emotional risks' for the mental development of young evacuee children separated from their mothers.[39] After the war, the importance of maternal devotion and maternal bonding became, in Sally Alexander's words, 'an orthodoxy of the postwar settlement'.[40] Tara Zahra has shown that they shaped the policies of the UN relief agencies responsible for Europe's displaced and refugee children after 1945. Drawing on concepts of reliable environments, attachment and maternal bonding, agencies prioritized the placement of children with foster families, rather than in group homes with fellow survivors. Yet in practice, many young Holocaust survivors (in particular) experienced this policy negatively, preferring life within a community of those who had experienced similar suffering to being placed with uncomprehending gentile families in the name of recreating maternal bonds.[41]

In the context of the 1940s and 1950s, with Cold War fears of Communist totalitarianism mixing with anxieties of a potential recurrence of fascism, the combination of child-centred, liberal-permissive pedagogy with a firm and orthodox family framework could appear crucial to the survival of democracy. Fascism and authoritarian personalities were pathologized; Mark Mazower has argued that this pathologization, based on depicting fascism and authoritarian personalities as something different, abnormal, Other, and curable, represented a comforting fiction that fed myths of the naturally democratic nature of British and American citizens.[42] Psychoanalysis, and the spread of psychoanalytic ideas to various state institutions, flourished in the US and Britain in this context.

The fact that psychoanalysis became so important in this ideological environment has appeared to suggest that there was something specifically postwar about the rise of psychoanalysis – especially so since this ideological edifice began to disintegrate in the late 1960s and early 1970s. The vision of the nuclear family and devoted mothers came under sustained attack from feminists, who contended that it helped to confine women to domesticity by generating feelings of guilt: if women went out to work, they risked generating separation traumas in their children, which might then be expressed in political extremism. In 1971, Gloria Steinem attacked Spock's book at the National Women's

Political Caucus as 'a symbol of male repression'.[43] In the context of social unrest, civil rights protests, and the Vietnam War, the post-war ideal of liberal American democracy seemed tarnished. 'Once upon a time', wrote Steinem, 'a Liberated Woman was somebody who had sex before marriage and a job afterward [while] a Liberated Zone was any foreign place lucky enough to have an American army in it. Both ideas seem antiquated now, and for pretty much the same reason: Liberation isn't exposure to the American values of Mom-and-apple-pie anymore ... it's the escape from them.'[44] The 1940s political context linking maternal devotion with the production of democratic citizens no longer held salience for 1970s feminists. Spock, who in 1972 ran for US president on a left-wing People's Party ticket, himself disavowed the gendered language of early editions of *Baby and Child Care*.

Translating psychoanalysis into French child-raising practices

Yet, it was at just this time that the woman who was in many ways Spock's French counterpart, Françoise Dolto, was finding a large-scale audience. Following a moderately successful phone-in programme on commercial radio in 1968–69, she published two books to critical acclaim in 1971. Above all, she rose to fame through her second radio show, on the state channel France Inter, entitled *Lorsque L'Enfant parait* ('When the Baby Comes'). This was broadcast daily, for 15 min, at 3.00 p.m., from 1976 to 1978, with Dolto responding to parenting and relationship problems submitted by listeners in letters. The show attracted a wide audience of parents (mainly mothers), grandparents, teenagers, teachers and medical professionals. It created a strong appetite for further books by Dolto. Her subsequent fame enabled her to set-up the 'Maison Verte', a Parisian early-years children's centre, partly staffed by psycho-analysts, which became the model for hundreds of similar centres (collectively called 'Lieux d'Accueil Enfants-Parents') across France. These remained a pillar of the French state's provision for young children and their parents into the twenty-first century.

Unlike Spock, Dolto did not write a systematic from-birth guide to the practicalities of raising a child. The closest French equivalent to *Baby and Child Care* was *J'élève mon enfant* (1965) by the journalist Laurence Pernoud, and its predecessor on pregnancy, *J'attends un enfant* (1956). Though bestsellers, these did not have Dolto's level of impact on child-rearing mentalities and ideologies; Pernoud's works summarized current scientific thinking rather than proposing new approaches. Dolto did resemble Spock in seeking to broaden the range of questions addressed by doctors and child-rearing experts, so to include many specifically psychological dilemmas: is it better for a child to sleep alone or in the same room as its parents? What should you tell a child if a close relative dies, or is sent to prison? What causes children to wet the bed or to have trouble sleeping? How do you deal with sibling rivalry? How do adolescents process parental divorce? What should parents tell their children about sex?

For Dolto the idea that babies were fully human beings from birth, desiring and autonomous subjects capable of independent thought and expression, was fundamental. She drew sharp contrasts between forms of parenting based on this principle, and those based on disciplinarian or behaviourist methods. A crying child should be spoken to 'gently, calmly – never shout "Shut up!" Because if you do that, the child will shut up, but will have still more anxiety, that cannot be manifested because of the need to submit to the mother's desire.'[45] When dealing with psychological dilemmas, Dolto's general principle was that children should be told the truth. In the event of a death in the family, parents should be honest with their children, explain the situation clearly, and admit their own shortcomings. Children might otherwise be left with powerful emotions and anxieties that they could not articulate or fit into a narrative that made sense of their experience. Such unresolved feelings could form the kernel of neuroses, or even long-term conditions such as schizophrenia or autism.

Language and communication, thus, occupied a central place in Dolto's vision and her advice to parents. This appeared timely in the intellectual context of French structuralism and the widespread idea that social and psychological structures could be analysed analogously to linguistic systems. Dolto's approach was less abstract than that of her colleague, Jacques Lacan, who famously argued that 'the Unconscious is structured like a language'. Dolto argued that all psychological ailments, and indeed most physical ones, could be traced to previous instances either of language or of non-verbal communication understood by the child's unconscious as a form of language. Physical symptoms should be understood as 'linguistic' in themselves, that is, as expressing something that the sufferer was otherwise struggling to verbalize. A young child who refused to eat or vomited up its food was most likely expressing its 'rejection' not of the food itself, but of something else, such as the family dynamics or perhaps the mother's anxiety around the subject of food.[46] Vomiting might in fact be a sign of a healthy refusal to conform to the mother's desires and schedules. Dolto's claim that both verbal and emotional language structure the unconscious was framed with sexual, religious and mystical overtones: 'language ... is the most germinating, the most inseminating thing in the heart and the symbolic understanding of the human being'.[47] The 'fruitfulness' of a communication was the measure of its success.

From such attitudes, Dolto also derived ideas about how to structure schools and other institutions. In her later years, she participated in the creation of a private school, and advised government committees on the psychological implications of *in vitro* fertilization and on the design of a science museum's children's section.[48] Dolto argued that schools should aid children to express their autonomy and creativity, with emphasis on crafts, skills, physical activity, performance and connecting with nature, rather than on facts and ideas.[49] She highlighted and denounced instances of disciplinarian punishment, such as the case of a teacher who taped pupils' mouths closed.[50] She sent her own children to Montessori schools, praised A.S. Neill's Summerhill as a model, and argued for schools to be run democratically, with heavy involvement from the pupils and attendance at 'traditional' classes made optional. The education ministry should be abolished and replaced with a more holistic 'youth and sport ministry' charged with forming both mind and body.[51] In the 1980s, she presented herself as a campaigner for children's rights, echoing other civil rights campaigns. She claimed that children were in effect a neglected minority in modern societies not designed for them, in which their needs and desires were not taken into account.[52] 'Parents educate their children like princes govern their peoples', she stated. 'Adults find scandalous the idea that children should be considered their equal.'[53]

Dolto, thus, claimed her approach as revolutionary and as a radical departure from the previously dominant paradigm. Many of her listeners and readers agreed. One listener wrote to Dolto in 1977 to say that 'it's such a shame I didn't know about you 20 years ago! I would have avoided so many difficulties. At that time, it was all about strict education, propriety, obedience! You had to "form" their character!'[54] Other correspondents praised Dolto for encouraging parents to show love and to communicate with their children as much as possible, contrasting this with the severe, distant attitudes of their own parents. Letters such as these illustrate the great receptivity of the French public to Dolto's ideas, and perhaps especially for the cultural shift towards less authoritarian attitudes that she embodied in the 1970s.

Dolto's listener situated the 'bad old days' of illiberal education in the 1950s, well after the point at which Spock's 'democratic' approach had taken off in the US. Yet Dolto (born 1908) was the same generation as Spock (born 1903) and had much in common with him in terms of background and ideological influence. Both came from upper-middle-class bourgeois families and from dominant cultural groups. Spock was from a White Anglo-Saxon Protestant family in New England; his father worked in the legal office of the New York and New Haven railroad, controlled by JP Morgan. Dolto came from the Catholic bourgeoisie of western Paris; her father ran a steel factory in Burgundy.[55] Both fathers were practical and to some degree self-made men, who had married women with more long-standing upper-class cultural credentials and a strong sense of class consciousness. Spock's mother Mildred disdained her husband's family and refused to go to their house; Dolto's mother Suzanne Marette, a monarchist and supporter of Action Française, likewise found her in-laws 'ordinary'.

The result, for both mothers, seems to have been a strong anxiety that their children's behaviour would 'fall' below the level expected of members of the higher class. Accordingly, each mother engaged in a committed policing of their children's comportment. Mildred Spock's 'effort to shape her children's character was so relentless that they lived in fear of her wrath'.[56] She believed in fresh air, strict diets and moral certainties. Her children had to call her 'mother' at all times and bow and doff their cap when respectable neighbours passed by. For her part, Dolto's mother Suzanne expected her daughters to conform to the demure, virginal, decorative role laid out for girls of her class. Dolto's pursuit of medical studies in the 1930s came at the cost of intense psychological tension with her family, who expected her to marry their chosen suitor and not pursue an independent career.[57] Both mothers were extremely anxious about their children's sexuality: Spock's mother banned him from dances attended by families she had not approved; Dolto's mother accused her of being a prostitute for mixing with male medical students.

For both Spock and Dolto, undergoing personal psychoanalysis in the 1930s was an opportunity to process difficult maternal conflicts, but also to question the kind of education and upbringing they had received. For Dolto, it further represented her entry point to the intellectual arena of child psychology and child development. It enabled her to encounter the same essential combination of ideas that Spock had found – the combination of the Freudian model of the mind with Dewey's educational liberalism and pedagogical concepts drawn from educational reformers.

In 1940s France, however, it was far from clear that psychoanalysis and democracy went together, as was claimed to be the case in the USA and Britain. From 1940 on, the political connotations of psychoanalysis began to follow a very different trajectory in France. In order to understand Dolto's career path, this history needs to be explored; the strength of French Catholicism, and the political implications of the Catholic vision of the family, emerge as particularly important factors. Dolto was mentored by two Catholic doctors, who combined psychoanalysis and liberal education with a strongly patriarchal vision of the family. If Spock enacted a similar combination – at least in the view of his feminist critics – for Dolto's mentors, this was not done in the name of defending democracy, but in the name of promoting a strong French national, gendered, and not necessarily democratic community, in a context where acceptance of the secular Third Republic was far from universal.

Interwar French child-rearing advice was closely associated both with political pronatalism after the demographic catastrophe of 1914–18, and with reasserting women's role as mothers following their expanded wartime economic role. Adolphe Pinard, a paediatrician with a seat in the National Assembly, popularized 'puériculture', defined as the teaching of the science of hygiene and infant care. His textbook on the subject was deployed in schools across France from 1923, when *puériculture* became part of the curriculum for all girls.[58] Early welfare state measures, such as crèches and family allowances, emerged in the context of the exhortation by Fernand Boverat, head of the National Alliance against Depopulation, that 'il faut faire naître' – we must have more births.[59] Catholics were vociferous and active both in the (officially secular) pronatalist campaign and in efforts to improve the quality of parenting. The École des Parents, a Paris institute in which parents could receive training and marriage counselling, was run by Catholic intellectuals and pro-family campaigners. Its leader was the bourgeois Catholic Marguerite Lebrun, known as Mme Vérine, later a staunch supporter of the Vichy regime's family policies.[60]

It was among Catholic nationalists that support for child-centred educational liberalism, and for the openness to psychoanalysis that generally accompanied it, were most likely to be found. France's small psychoanalytic movement in the 1930s was a curious coalition of xenophobic Catholic male doctors alongside a number of female and/or immigrant Jewish analysts. The leading exponent of the synthesis between psychoanalysis and liberal educational theory was Édouard Pichon, a medical doctor, scholar of linguistics, and activist for the far-right, monarchist group Action Française. His 1936 manual le *Développement psychique* de *l'enfant et de l'adolescent* was a bestseller. Like the British and American thinkers discussed earlier, Pichon insisted that a baby is fully human: 'a complete being with a full experience of life and its joys and sorrows'.[61] The first duty of parents was to ensure that their offspring had 'gentle, full and happy' childhoods. Pichon condemned 'systematically strict paternal authoritarianism, slapping and smacking, upbringing without tenderness, and avoidable exiles in boarding schools'.[62] He approvingly cited Melanie Klein's technique of using children's free play to help interpret their mental distress. He encouraged parents to talk to their children as much as possible and not treat them like 'little unconscious objects'.[63] At the same time, Pichon argued from psychoanalytic and medical authority that the optimum psychic development of the child required certain familial conditions. Like Spock's, Pichon's vision presupposed a dedicated, devoted mother who would put her children's interests above her own. Parental separation, widowhood, divorce, remarriage, illegitimacy and being an only child were all dangerous to psychic equilibrium. Parents should also not abdicate responsibility in favour of a nanny or governess, especially a foreign one, since this would prevent the child from 'making contact with the customs of his nation'.[64]

Pichon espoused a concept borrowed from René Laforgue, the Catholic founder of the French psychoanalytic movement: that of the 'family neurosis', according to which children's disturbances were often the result of other family members' neuroses. Laforgue wrote in 1927 that 'a neurosis can transmit itself via family tradition, exactly as civilisation transmits itself'.[65] For Laforgue, the responsibility for a 'family complex' usually lay with or could be traced back to women, especially 'the influence that an unbalanced mother has on her child'.[66] In 1935, Laforgue explicitly linked the concept of family neurosis to women's sexual 'frigidity', where the origins of numerous 'neurotic family symptoms' should be sought.[67] Frigidity, defined as the lack of appropriate release of women's sexual energies, could lead to those energies being expressed in 'a certain virility' that pushed women to try and succeed professionally, or in an overly strong attachment to a child.[68] In either case, the child would suffer the consequences. The definition of 'unbalanced' women included feminists and indeed any women uncomfortable with being confined to the role of wife and mother.

Pichon and Laforgue, who both gave talks at the École des Parents in the 1930s, were the key intellectual influences on Dolto: Laforgue as her analyst, Pichon as the supervisor of her thesis, completed in 1939. The continuity between Pichon's and Dolto's ideas on communication and punishment is apparent. Dolto's relationship with Laforgue is more paradoxical: given the theories he championed, it seems likely that her parents selected him as her analyst in the hope that he would 'cure' her desire for a professional career. Laforgue did not do this, but Dolto later echoed, in modified form, his ideas on the family neurosis and the link between women's sexual attitudes and children's mental disturbances. For Dolto and her protégée Maud Mannoni (writing in 1965), the archetypal pathogenic family could be summarized by the labels 'depressive mother', 'passive', 'resigned' or 'absent' father, and 'objectified child'.[69] In other words, depressed mothers and unimposing fathers were responsible for creating passive, disturbed children, who responded by displaying autistic or schizophrenic behaviours. A family in which the mother was too strong a personality, or too possessive of the child to the exclusion of the father's Law, was toxic. 'Any substitution of the father's role by the mother is pathogenic', Dolto wrote.[70]

In the 1930s, the views of Laforgue and Pichon (who died in January 1940) were balanced within the psychoanalytic movement by analysts to their political left, such as Rudolph Loewenstein, Marie Bonaparte and Paul Schiff. These analysts' research centred on sexology and the adult ego rather than family neuroses and guilt, another Catholic-inflected theme promoted by Laforgue.[71] However, this political balance was altered by the Nazi Occupation, which pushed the Jewish and foreign analysts into exile. The result was that in the immediate post-war period, as Spock's book was appearing in New York and the influence of Winnicott and Bowlby was ascendant in Britain, French psychoanalysis had a distinctly Catholic and conservative character. From 1946 until the *Revue Française de Psychanalyse* resumed in 1949, the main journal for psychoanalytic thought was *Psyché*, which aimed to bring Catholicism and psychoanalysis together. The analysts who published there, including Dolto, were generally former analysands of Laforgue.

In 1946, Laforgue and tried for collaboration for attempting to 'aryanise' the Parisian Psychoanalytic Society and co-operate with Nazis in 1940–41. Early *Psyché* editions made substantial reference to Alexis Carrel, the eugenicist scientist and creator of a Vichy-funded think-tank, the Centre for the Study of Human Problems, whose 'Centre for the Mother and the Child' hired Dolto in 1943. The Centre Claude

Bernard, which from 1946 offered publicly funded child psychoanalysis, was the brain-child of Georges Mauco, a racist demographer and former member of a fascist party. In the later 1940s, the charge from the French Communist Party that psychoanalysis was a doctrine working 'against the forces of democracy and peace', thus, had a certain resonance.[72]

Researching in the early 1950s, Serge Moscovici found that most French people, especially in working-class areas, considered psychoanalysis 'a fashionable treatment for society women', and did not associate it to the welfare state.[73] Though this was also a widely held view in the US, it was more contested there. Joshua Loth Liebman's 1946 book *Peace of Mind*, showing how psychoanalysis could supplement religious faith and healing, was a popular bestseller. *Time* magazine had a 'consistent commitment to keeping the American public well informed about developments within and around ... psychoanalysis', including explaining in 1946 how the National Advisory Mental Health Council was spending millions expanding the provision of psychoanalytic psychiatry.[74]

It would take until the later 1960s for the political associations of psychoanalysis to change substantially in France. In the intervening period, as Sandrine Garcia has shown, the key political debate concerning French family policy was over the continued illegality of contraception – another important point of contextual difference from the US and Britain.[75] Interwar campaigns to legalize contraception had failed in the face of France's birth shortage and the political strength of pronatalist and familialist currents. Legal contraception appeared a more attainable goal in the context of the baby boom, but also because of the weakened post-war credibility of the medical establishment.

The French doctors' association, the Ordre des Médecins, created under Vichy in 1942, remained dominated by conservative, xenophobic and antifeminist currents; it opposed contraception. By contrast, the doctors and journalists who led the French Family Planning Movement were frequently ex-Resisters, many from Protestant or Jewish backgrounds. They saw the battle to defeat medical moralists and the Catholic Church as a continuation of the wartime struggle. Their campaign sought to increase women's rights by replacing the emphasis on large families – the 'famille nombreuse' – with that of 'happy' ones, leading to the creation of the Association Maternité Heureuse in 1956.

According to one of the movement's founders, contraception would contribute to 'women's dignity and social promotion'.[76] For Simone de Beauvoir, whose *The Second Sex* (1949) acted as a foundational text for the movement, women would only be free to play a fuller role in society when they had birth control options beyond illegal abortion. Some psychoanalysts, including child analysts (but not Dolto), joined the cause, arguing that avoiding unwanted pregnancies would result in happier children. Forcing women to sacrifice themselves to an unwanted child would likely result in negative psychological consequences for that child; avoiding the trauma of clandestine abortions was a good thing for all concerned.[77] After the National Assembly legalized contraception in 1967, similar arguments were advanced in the campaign to legalize abortion, which succeeded in 1975, 2 years after the Roe v. Wade judgement affirming the right to abortion in the US.

By this time, psychoanalysis had become a major cultural force in France, stimulated in particular by the charisma and intellectual vitality of Jacques Lacan. Lacan broadened the social and political appeal of psychoanalysis, convincing a number of left-wing intellectuals that they should be interested in (his interpretation of) Freud. Lacan sought alliances with radical critics of existing institutional practices, for example in psychiatry and education; his seminars overlapped with contemporary avant-garde philosophy. A number of left-wing activists turned to psychoanalysis in the aftermath of May 1968, as a means of deepening their political understanding as well as their personal self-discovery. This was true of some women's rights campaigners, most notably Antoinette Fouque, leader of the Mouvement de Libération des Femmes, who was in analysis with Lacan between 1969 and 1974. Feminist writer Luce Irigaray made use of Lacanian concepts and offered qualified praise for Dolto, in her 1977 book *This Sex Which Is Not One*.[78] Feminists critical of psychoanalysis, such as those of the Front Homosexuel d'Action Révolutionnaire, remained marginal with respect to French culture as a whole.

By the mid-1970s, however, and despite Lacan's best efforts, there was a sense that avant-garde intellectual culture was beginning to move beyond psychoanalysis and its emphasis on the domestic sphere. Gilles Deleuze and Félix Guattari's *Anti-Oedipus* (1972) – Guattari having previously been an enthusiastic Lacanian – was an important watershed moment in this context. Another was the disruption of a radio debate on 'the painful problem of homosexuality' – featuring a psychoanalyst and a priest and moderated by Ménie Grégoire, an agony aunt who employed psychoanalytic ideas – by gay rights' activists in 1971.[79] If these events suggested that psychoanalysis was no longer at the cutting edge of intellectual culture, they perhaps thereby helped to make psychoanalysis more attractive to mainstream 1970s audiences, to people who still welcomed its focus on domesticity, and were put off by radical egalitarianism and identity politics.

This new political status for psychoanalysis in France partly explains how Dolto, finally, found a large public audience in the 1970s, when she was invited to broadcast in a prime slot on state radio. This context also helps explain how Dolto could present herself as radical and innovative, despite the fact that many of her ideas, as indicated, originated in interwar Catholic pro-family and anti-feminist thinking. After 1968, France was receptive to discourses claiming that the traditional way of doing things was in need of thorough revision. Dolto's emphasis on the rights of children and adolescents seemed to place her on the side of the 1968-era attacks on France's old guard. Yet at the same time, the fact that traces of the interwar origins of her thinking were visible in Dolto's 1970s persona contributed to the breadth of her appeal. As a Catholic mother of three and a grandmother, keen on neither abortion nor feminism, she offered Catholic and conservative audiences a psychoanalysis that had something to offer them too. In the context of rapidly declining church attendance, Dolto offered a new source of reassurance and guidance on a wide range of personal issues. The 1970s can be seen as a period in which some parts of the French public sought out ideas and approaches which attacked traditional sources of moral(izing) authority, while others sought to restrain the extent of social change and the disruption of established family structures and gender roles. Dolto's success came from her ability to speak to large sections of both groups. Her public appeal could, thus, be a truly national one, transcending partisan divides.

Furthermore, as Garcia has argued, Dolto's emphasis on the rights of the child, as opposed to the rights of mothers, can be understood as part of the beginning of a cultural backlash against the successes of the women's rights movement and against the more radical feminist movements of the 1970s. Beyond abortion, these successes included some funding of contraception through national health insurance, and the replacement of the *allocation* de *salaire unique*, a benefit for families with one wage earner and, thus, an inducement to women to stay at home, with a generalized childcare benefit that accrued also to mothers who worked outside the home.[80] Dolto shifted the focus onto what psychoanalytic theory indicated was best for the child. She argued that this consisted of living in happy, fertile (or 'fruitful', in her Christianized language) nuclear families with a strong paternal presence. In doing so, she presented defenders of the 'traditional' family with a new way to package orthodox patriarchal gender roles, showing that the languages of psychoanalysis, then seen as cutting-edge science, and of the civil rights movement, could be turned to this purpose. The rhetorical emphasis of her discourse was on attacking authoritarian, hierarchical, disciplinarian and psychologically insensitive modes of upbringing. The apparent political progressiveness of this stance, and the deference that was generally shown towards Dolto's decades of clinical experience as an analyst, helped to shield her views from criticism of the patriarchal implications. Nonetheless, feminists did sometimes take Dolto to task, as when Christine Delphy attacked her on television in 1985 for her idea that women who underwent an abortion should pay a small 'symbolic fine' so as to avoid the 'banalisation' of abortion.

Dolto's popular interventions in these debates had far-reaching implications. In the 1970s and 1980s, she was consulted on family policy and bioethics by successive governments of opposing political stances. Camille Robcis has shown how her views influenced politicians from across the spectrum who successfully fought to keep homosexual parenting rights out of the 1999 PACS civil partnership legislation, and in debates in over the 1994 bioethics laws, which (until 2011) allowed only couples married for over 2 years to access assisted reproduction.[81] Dolto's daughter Catherine, a paediatrician and champion of her mother's intellectual legacy, has offered support to La Manif Pour Tous – a campaign group and political party-based around opposition to gay marriage and defence of the 'traditional family'. In 2015, she argued that the legalization of surrogate pregnancies, for example, would lead to 'barbarism' and 'violence' by ignoring the importance of the unconscious psychological transmissions that happen during pregnancy.[82]

Conclusion

In 1940s Britain and the US, the identification of psychoanalytic theories of child development with the formation of democratic personalities went hand in hand with the pathologization of fascism and authoritarian personalities. Early childhood interventions by experts would help ensure immunity from anti-democratic takeover; upholding and spreading democratic and humanist ideas into everyday life would ensure the future stability of the polity.

In France, however, the experience of 1940–44 made clear that previously ordinary people could be tempted, if not by Nazism as such, then at least by collaboration and acquiescence with Occupation. Indeed, several of the psychological experts who in a different context might have made that diagnosis had themselves been tempted; given this, it was not really possible to present psychoanalysis as central to the preservation of democracy. Dolto herself never went as far as Laforgue, but did publish two articles in the heavily Vichyite and German-approved magazine *Vrai* in

1941, and worked for a pro-Vichy think-tank, the Centre de la Mère et de l'Enfant, in 1943.[83]

But there is also the consideration that in France it was the events of 1968, rather than of 1939–45, that brought about a thorough public questioning of the cultural values that informed French discourses on the family. There, it was in the 1970s, rather than the 1940s, when the combination of liberal, child-centred pedagogy with an insistence on the importance of 'traditional' families and gender roles – suitably sublimated into the language of psychoanalysis – held the most resonance. By the 1970s, it was less democracy itself that was at stake than the balance of power and rights between different social groups. Dolto's focus on the 'rights of children' helped to move French parenting and educational culture away from disciplinarian norms that persisted in some quarters well beyond 1945. It was also, in practice, an argument against radical feminism and gay rights and in favour of 'traditional family' structures. The democratic humanism of Spock, Winnicott and Bowlby also functioned to that end, but their association with the immediate post-war period allowed their assumptions to be dismantled by the mid-1970s. By this time, Spock himself had largely accepted the arguments of his feminist critics. A key difference with enduring consequences for French society is that Dolto's association with the later period and with 1968-era radicalism allowed her to have an impact on French social policy debates that resonated arguably into the twenty-first century – without the older, Catholic, patriarchal assumptions inherent in her thought necessarily being widely discussed.

This article has attempted to demonstrate the importance of assessing the impact of contingent contextual factors in shaping the public reception of specific applications of broader theories: in this case, the application of psychoanalysis to child rearing. As Herzog has argued, in the post-war decades, psychoanalysis could have 'both normative-conservative and socially critical implications', depending largely on the surrounding cultural environment.[84] The most interesting recent historiography on psychoanalysis, such as the works of Herzog, Shapira and Alexander cited in this article, is precisely that which seeks to situate it more deeply in different historical and national-cultural contexts. Such work makes it easier to see how psychoanalysis, which may appear to be ahistorical in its view of the human psyche, has in fact been dynamic and adaptable to evolving societal conditions. The transition in the historiography of psychoanalysis from insider-histories into broader cultural history presents opportunities to focus on sites and practices, such as child rearing that illustrate interactions between ideas and ideologies, state policy, and patterns of economic and social change.

Notes

1. The number of buildings and institutions named for Dolto reached 230 by 1999. Recent examples include a new school near Eurodisney in 2013, and a Gentilly hospital unit in 2014.
2. D. Pleux, *Génération Dolto* (Paris: Odile Jacob, 2008).
3. S. Fishman, *From Vichy to the Sexual Revolution: Gender and Family Life in Postwar France* (Oxford: Oxford University Press, 2017).
4. D. Herzog, *Cold War Freud: Psychoanalysis in an Age of Catastrophes* (Cambridge : Cambridge University Press, 2017), p. 2.

5. Herzog, ibid.; M. Shapira, *The War Inside: Psychoanalysis, Total War, and the Making of the Democratic Self in Postwar Britain* (New York: Cambridge University Press, 2013); C. Robcis, *The Law of Kinship: Anthropology, Psychoanalysis, and the Family in France* (Ithaca, NY: Cornell University Press, 2013); T. Zahra, '"The Psychological Marshall Plan": Displacement, Gender, and Human Rights after World War II', *Central European History* 44/1 (2011), 37–62.

6. See e.g. C. Urwin & E. Sharland, 'From Bodies to Minds in Childcare Literature: Advice to Parents in Inter-war Britain', in R. Cooter (Ed.) *In the Name of the Child: Health and Welfare in England, 1880–1940* (London: Routledge, 1992), pp. 174–199.

7. E.g. W. Graebner, 'The Unstable World of Benjamin Spock: Social Engineering in a Democratic Culture, 1917–1950', *The Journal of American History* 67/3 (1980), pp. 612–629; T. Maier, *Dr. Spock: An American Life* (New York: Harcourt Brace, 2003); J. Bourke, *Fear: A Cultural History* (London: Virago, 2006).

8. L.E. Holt, *The Care and Feeding of Children* (New York: D. Appleton, 1894); J.B. Watson, *Psychological Care of Infant and Child* (New York: Allen & Unwin, 1928); Truby King, *Feeding and Care of Baby* (London: Macmillan, 1913).

9. On Isaacs see S. Bar-Haim, 'The liberal playground: Susan Isaacs, psychoanalysis and progressive education in the interwar era' *History of the Human Sciences* 30/1 (2017), pp. 94–117; and M. Shapira, 'Speaking Kleinian': Susan Isaacs as Ursula Wise and the Inter-War Popularisation of Psychoanalysis', *Medical History* 61/4 (2017), pp. 525–547.

10. P.J. Graham, *Susan Isaacs: A Life Freeing the Minds of Children* (London: Karnac, 2009), p. 98; Idem., 'Susan Isaacs and the Malting House School', *Journal of Child Psychotherapy* 34/1 (2008), pp. 5–22.

11. A.C. Aldrich & M.M. Aldrich, *Babies are Human Beings: An Interpretation of Growth* (New York: Macmillan, 1938). See C. Hardyment, *Dream Babies: Child Care from Locke to Spock* (London: Jonathan Cape, 1983), pp. 213–220.

12. S. Alexander, 'Primary Maternal Preoccupation: D.W. Winnicott and Social Democracy in Mid-Twentieth-Century Britain', in S. Alexander & B. Taylor (Eds) *History and Psyche: Culture, Psychoanalysis, and the Past* (New York: Palgrave Macmillan, 2012), pp. 149–172, ref. p. 158.

13. Maier, *Dr. Spock, op. cit.*, Ref. 7, p. 106.

14. A. Prost, *Éducation, société et politiques: une histoire de l'enseignement en France de 1945 à nos jours* (Paris: Seuil, 1997); M. Thomson, *Psychological Subjects: Identity, Culture, and Health in Twentieth-Century Britain* (Oxford: Oxford University Press, 2006); E. Shorter, *The Making of the Modern Family* (London: Collins, 1975); E. Zaretsky, *Political Freud: A History* (New York: Columbia University Press, 2015).

15. Prost, *Éducation, société et politiques, op. cit.*, pp. 26–27.

16. S. Isaacs, *The Nursery Years* (London: Routledge, 1929), pp. 2–3.

17. Isaacs, ibid., pp. 2–3.

18. Quoted in Hardyment, *Dream Babies, op. cit.*, Ref. 11, p. 159.

19. M. Shapira, 'Psychoanalytic criminology, childhood and the democratic self', in M. Ffytche & D. Pick (Eds), *Psychoanalysis in the Age of Totalitarianism* (Abingdon: Routledge, 2016), pp. 73–86.

20. M. Shapira, *The War Inside: Psychoanalysis, Total War, and the Making of the Democratic Self in Postwar Britain* (New York: Cambridge University Press, 2013), p. 1.

21. S. Alexander, 'D.W. Winnicott and the social democratic vision', in Ffytche & Pick (Eds) *Psychoanalysis in the Age of Totalitarianism*, pp. 114–130, Ref. 19, p. 117.

22. Graebner, 'The Unstable World of Benjamin Spock', *op. cit.*, Ref. 7, p. 615.

23. B. Spock, *Baby and Child Care* (London: Bodley Head, 1958), pp. 405–406.

24. Graebner, 'The Unstable World of Benjamin Spock', *op. cit.*, Ref. 7, p. 613.

25. J. Dewey, *Democracy and Education* (New York: Macmillan, 1916), p. 93.

26. N. Noddings, 'Dewey's philosophy of education: a critique from the perspective of care theory', in M. Cochran (Ed) *The Cambridge Companion to Dewey* (Cambridge: Cambridge University Press, 2010), pp. 265–287, here p. 279.
27. Dewey, 'Freedom and Culture', in J. Boydston (Ed) *John Dewey: The Later Works, 1925–1952, vol.13, 1938–39* (Carbondale: Southern Illinois University Press, 1987), p. 187.
28. Noddings, 'Dewey's philosophy of education', *op. cit.*, Ref. 26, p. 280.
29. Maier, *Dr. Spock, op. cit.*, Ref. 7, pp. 97–98.
30. L. Farley, 'Analysis on Air: A Sound History of Winnicott in Wartime', *American Imago* 69/4 (2012), pp. 449–471.
31. Spock, *Baby and Child Care, op. cit.*, p. 405.
32. Bar-Haim, 'The liberal playground', *op. cit*, p. 96.
33. Maier, *Dr. Spock, op. cit.*, Ref. 7, p. 102.
34. Spock, *Baby and Child Care, op. cit.*, Ref. 23, p. 570.
35. Graebner, 'The Unstable World of Benjamin Spock', *op. cit.*, Ref. 7, pp. 619–622.
36. Spock, *Baby and Child Care, op. cit.*, Ref. 23, p. 365.
37. Spock, *Ibid.*, p. 321.
38. M. Shapira, 'Psychoanalysts on the Radio – Domestic citizenship and motherhood in postwar Britain', in J. Regulska & B.G. Smith (Eds) *Women and Gender in Postwar Europe: From Cold War to European Union* (Abingdon: Routledge, 2012), pp.71–86, ref. pp. 81–82.
39. Alexander, 'D.W. Winnicott and the social democratic vision', *op. cit.*, Ref. 21, pp. 124–125.
40. Alexander, *Ibid.*, p. 127.
41. Zahra, 'Psychological Marshall Plan', *op. cit.*, Ref. 5.
42. M. Mazower, 'Ideas that fed the beast of fascism are flourishing today', *Financial Times* 07/11/2016.
43. Maier, *Dr. Spock, op.cit.*, Ref. 7, p. 353.
44. G. Steinem, 'After Black Power, Women's Liberation', *New York Magazine*, April 4 1969.
45. F. Dolto, *Lorsque l'enfant paraît*, vol. I (Paris: Seuil, 1977), p. 144.
46. Dolto, ibid., p. 84.
47. F. Dolto, *Tout est langage* (Paris: Gallimard, 1987), p. 50.
48. See F. d'Ortoli & M. Amram, *L'École avec Françoise Dolto*: le rôle Du désir dans l'éducation (Paris: Hatier, 1989).
49. F. Dolto, La *Cause* Des *enfant*s (Paris: Robert Laffont, 1985), pp. 399–434.
50. Archives Françoise Dolto 'LLP 14', week 43.
51. Dolto, *Cause* Des *enfants, op. cit.*, Ref. 49, p. 410.
52. F. Dolto, La *Cause* Des *adolescents* (Paris: Robert Laffont, 1988).
53. Dolto, *Cause* Des *enfants, op. cit.*, Ref. 49, p. 13.
54. Archives Françoise Dolto 'LLP 9'. Formerly a private collection, in 2015–16 these archives were moved to the French Archives Nationales.
55. Details taken from Dolto's autobiographical works *Enfances* (Paris: Seuil, 1988) and *Autoportrait d'une psychanalyste 1934–1988* (Paris: Seuil, 1989), also C. Percheminier (Ed) *Lettres de jeunesse: correspondance, 1913–1938* (Paris; Gallimard, 2003), and Y. Potin (Ed) *Françoise Dolto, Archives de l'intime* (Paris: Gallimard, 2008).
56. Maier, *Dr Spock, op. cit.*, Ref. 7, pp. 8–10.
57. See I. Grellet & C. Kruse, Des *Jeunes Filles Exemplaires: Dolto, Beauvoir et Zaza* (Paris: Hachette, 2004).
58. L. Clark, *Schooling the Daughters of Marianne: Textbooks and the Socialization of Girls in Modern French Primary Schools* (Albany, NY: State University of New York Press, 1984), pp. 82–83.
59. F. Boverat, 'Il faut faire naître', *Revue de l'Alliance Nationale pour l'Accroissement* de La *Population Française* 143 (1924), pp. 163–171.
60. A. Ohayon, 'L'École des parents ou l'éducation des enfants éclairée par la psychologie (1929–1946)', *Bulletin* de *psychologie* 449 (2000), pp. 635–642; F. Muel-Dreyfus, *Vichy et*

l'éternel féminin: contribution à une sociologie politique de *l'ordre* Des *corps* (Paris: Seuil, 1996), pp. 181–184.

61. E. Pichon, le *Développement psychique* de *l'enfant et* de *l'adolescent. Évolution normale, pathologie, traitement. Manuel d'étude* (Paris: Masson, 1936), p. 25.

62. Pichon, ibid., p. 260–261.

63. Pichon, ibid., p. 277.

64. Pichon, *Ibid.*, p. 276.

65. R. Laforgue, 'Schizophrénie et schizonoia', *Revue Française* de *Psychanalyse* 1/I (1927), pp. 6–23.

66. Laforgue, *Ibid.*, p. 11.

67. R. Laforgue, 'A propos de la frigidité de la femme', *Revue Française* de *Psychanalyse* 8/II (1935), pp. 217–226; ref. p. 222.

68. R. Laforgue, 'La Névrose Familiale', *Revue Française* de *Psychanalyse* 9/III (1936), pp. 327–360, ref. p. 344.

69. M. Mannoni, le *Premier Rendez-vous avec* le *psychanalyste* (Paris: Gallimard, 1965), p. 56.

70. Dolto, preface to Mannoni, ibid., p. 22–23.

71. A. Ohayon, 'L'émergence d'un mouvement sexologique français (1929–1939), entre hygiéniste, eugénisme et psychanalyse', *PSN – psychiatrie, sciences humaines, neurosciences* 1/4 (2003), pp. 50–61.

72. L. Bonnafé et al, 'La Psychanalyse, idéologie réactionnaire', La *Nouvelle Critique* (juin 1949), pp. 57–72.

73. S. Moscovici, La *Psychanalyse: son image et son public* (Paris: PUF, 1976), p. 314.

74. Herzog, *Cold War Freud, op. cit.*, Ref. 4, p. 33.

75. S. Garcia, *Mères sous influence*: de La *cause* Des *femmes à* La *cause* Des *enfants* (Paris: La Découverte, 2011).

76. Garcia, *Ibid.*, p. 42.

77. Garcia, *Ibid.*, p. 91ff.

78. L. Irigaray, *This Sex Which Is Not One*, trans. Catherine Porter with Carolyn Burke, (Ithaca: Cornell University Press, 1985), p. 63.

79. On this episode see J. Mowitt, *Radio: Essays in Bad Reception* (Stanford: University of California Press, 2011), pp. 105ff; S. Gunther, *The Elastic Closet: A History of Homosexuality in France, 1942-present* (Basingstoke: Palgrave Macmillan, 2008), ch. 2.

80. See Robcis, *Law of Kinship, op. cit.*, Ref. 5, p. 153.

81. Robcis, *Ibid.*, ch. 6.

82. C. Dolto, 'GPA: Nous préparons la barbarie à venir', La *Manif Pour Tous* 51, 06/05/2015, http://la-manif-pour-tous-51.blogspot.co.uk/2015/05/cdolto-gpa-nous-preparons-la-barbarie.html.

83. C. Dolto, 'Ayez votre médecin de famille', *Vrai* 3, 15 novembre 1941, pp. 28–29; C. Dolto, 'Nos enfants. Savez-vous leur parler?', *Vrai* 4, 1 décembre 1941, p. 23.

84. Herzog, *Cold War Freud, op. cit.*, Ref. 4, p. 1.

Disclosure statement

No potential conflict of interest was reported by the authors.

Index

abortion: Reform Party (Canada) 61; *Roe v. Wade* 30; USA 33–34, 35
adjacent concepts, ideology studies 48
The Adventures of Augie March (Bellow) 70
African-American civil rights 33, 83–84; dehumanization of 84
Agenda, Alternatives, and Public policies (Kingdon) 31–32
Aldrich, Mary 91–92
Alexander, Sally 95
America as a Civilization (Lerner) 81
American Civilization (James) 81
American Literature: A Journal of Literary History, Criticism and Bibliography 75
American Renaissance: Art and Expression in Age of Emerson and Whitman (Matthiessen) 70–71
American studies movement 73
America's Coming of Age (Van Wyck) 75
Anderson, Benedict 19, 74
Anglican Church of Canada 37
anti-authoritarianism, child-rearing advice 90–91
anti-communism 35, 77; Boorstin 81
Anti-Oedipus (Guattari) 102
anti-representational representative claims 57
anti-Soviet role, USA 82–83
aspiration, freedom and 17
Austria, presidential elections 2016 2

Baby and Child Care (Spock) 93, 94
Baldwin, James 83–84, 85–86
Banal Nationalism (Billig) 19
Bar-Haim, Shaul 94–95
Barzun, Jacques 70
behaviourist approaches, child-rearing 91–92
Bellow, Saul 70
Billig, Michael 19
Bonaparte, Marie 100
Bonikowski, Bart 50
Boorstein, Daniel 80, 81
Brexit referendum (UK) 2, 13, 24
Brooks, Van Wyck 75–76
Buchanan, Pat 35
Buckley, William F. 32–33

Burkean conservatism *see* traditionalism
Burlingham, Dorothy 91
Bush, George H. W. 35

Campaign Life Canada 37–38
Campaign Life Coalition 39
Canada: direct democracy and tax reforms 58–63; LGBTQ rights 37, 39; social conservatism 36–41; USA, influence on 40–41
Canadian Conservative and Reform Alliance 62–63
capital punishment, Reform Party (Canada) 61
Carter, Jimmy 55
Centre Claude Bernard 100–101
Chakrabarty, Dipesh 6
charismatic leaders, populism 52–53
Charlottetown Accord, Reform Party (Canada) and 59
child development, psychoanalysis 103–104
childhood determinism 91–92
child-rearing advice 89–107; anti-authoritarianism 90–91; behaviourist approaches 91–92; France 96–103; hygienist approaches 91–93; national discrepancies 90; psychoanalysis 93, 95–96, 101; psychoanalytic theory 6–7; totalitarian ideology 92; USA and Britain 91–96
citizens, self-representation 57
Cold War 77; end of 35
The Common Sense Book of Baby and Child Care (Spock) 91
communication, Dolto's child-rearing 97
communism 12–13
community 19–21; imagined 19–20; interpretation 12–13; national communities 23; opposition, lack of 12–13
conceptual morphology 3
conservatism: free market conservatism 28, 29; fusionist conservatives 33; social conservatism *see* social conservatism
Conservative Caucus 58
conspiracy theories 23–24
constructivist ideology analysis, Freeden 53

constructivist theorization, political representation (Saward) 53, 63
contemporary populism 50–51
contraception, France 101
Cowley, Malcolm 76
critiques of failed representation, populist politics 47
Croce, Benedetto 6, 73
Croly, Herbert 75
crowd-sourced political ideas 9–26; diaries 12; non-specialist discourse 11–13; *see also* Massive Open Online Course (MOOC)
culture: centred notion of 76–77; mid-century Americanism 72–73; national culture 83–86; nation building of USA 73–78
Culture and Society (Williams) 76

Daedalus, Stephen 85
de Beauvoir, Simone 90, 101
dehumanization of the Negro 84
Deleuze, Gilles 102
Delphy, Christine 103
Democracy and Education (Spock) 94
'de-radicalization', left-wing writers 77
de Tocqueville, Alexis 80
Développementpsychique de l'enfant et de l'adolescent (Pichon) 99
Dewey, John 6, 90; democracy definition 94
Dickstein, Samuel 78
Dies, Martin 78
direct democracy 56; Canada 58–63; North America 46–69; popularity of 64; Reform Party (Canada) 61; tax revolts 54; USA 54–58
discourse analysis 3; Freeden's morphological approach and 4–5
Dolto, Françoise 7, 89, 90, 96–103; children as human beings 96–97; Laforgue and 100; psychoanalysis 98; rights of the child 102–103

economic equality, justice 17–18
economic inequality 22
economic regulation, post-war welfare state and 29
educational liberalism, French child-rearing 99
ego-documents 12
elected representation 49
Engels, Friedrich 2–3
English-Speaking Justice (Rawls) 30
equality: definition by Reform Party (Canada) 62; economic equality 17–18; gender equality amendment 34; justice and 21–22; marriage equality *see* same-sex marriage/marriage equality
Equal Rights Amendment to US Constitution 33–34, 35
ethnic groups, community 19

Falwell, Jerry 34, 35

Family Book (St Aubyn) 91–92
family complex, French child-rearing 100
Farley, Lisa 94
fascism, communism *vs.* 12–13
The Fire Next Time (Baldwin) 85–86
Fishman, Sarah 90
flexible ideology 27
Focus on the Family (Canada) 38
Fouque, Antoinette 102
France: child-rearing advice 96–103; psychoanalysis 101–102
Frank, Lawrence K 93
Freeden, Michael 47; constructivist ideology analysis 53; ideational formations 31; ideological analysis by interpretative model 63; ideology studies 47–48; intellectual history 28; political speech intensification 52
Freeden's morphological approach 41–42; discourse analysis and 4–5; North American conservatism 5; populist politics 50; social conservatism 27
freedom 14–17, 50; Brexit referendum (UK) advertising 24; definitions 13; images of 16–17; interpretation 12–13; justice and 21–22; opposition, lack of 12–13
free market conservatism 28, 29
Free Trade Agreement (1988 Canada) 39
French Family Planning Movement 101
Freunet, Célestin 90
Friedman, Milton 29, 54
frigidity 100
Froebel, Friedrich 90
From the Heart of Europe (Matthiessen) 72
Front Homosexuel d'Action Révolutionnaire 102
functional streams, government agencies 32
fusionist conservatives 33

Gann, Paul 55, 58
Garcia, Sandrine 101
gendered role models 95
gender equality amendment (USA) 34
general form of the representative claim (Saward) 49
Genius of American Politics (Boorstein) 80
Goldwater, Barry 33, 54
Graebner, William 93
Grant, George 30
Grégoire, Ménie 102
Gregory, Horace 81
Guattari, Félix 102

Harper, Steven 39, 63
Hartz, Louis 80
Hayek, F. A. 29, 31
Hofstader, Richard 80
Hollywood Ten 78–79
Holt, Luther Emett 91

House Committee on Un-American Activities
(HUAC) 78
Howe, Irving 77–78, 82
Hubbell, Jay B. 75
hygienist approaches, child-rearing 91–93

iconography 22
ideological evolution 31–32
ideology: action, recognition of 3–4; Americanism
of 85–86; Freeden studies 47–48; interpretative
analysis model (Freeden) 63; morphological
conceptual mapping 51; political ideas and 2–3;
recent methods of analysis 3
images 22–23; community 20–21, 23; freedom
16–17, 22–23; justice 18–19
imagined communities 19–20
Imagined Communities (Anderson) 74
injustice: justice *vs.* 17; specific examples 18
intellectuals, rise of in USA 75
internal barrier, freedom to 14–15
interpretative model, ideological analysis
(Freeden) 63
Irigaray, Luce 102
Isaacs, Susan 90, 91, 94

James, C. L. R. 81
Jarvis, Howard 54; Proposition 13, 54–58; tax
revolts 46
J'attends un enfant (Pernoud) 96
J'élèvemon enfant (Pernoud) 96
justice 17–19; equality and 21–22; financial
equality 17; freedom and 21–22; interpretation
12–13; opposition, lack of 12–13; post-war
justice 18; *see also* injustice

Kazin, Alfred 76
Kingdon, John 31–32
King, Truby 91
Klein, Melanie 91, 99
Kronenberg, Louis 83
Ku Klux Klan 78–79

Lacan, Jacques 97, 101–102
Lafourgue, René 99–101; Dolto and 100
language, Dolto's child-rearing 97
left-wing writers, de-radicalization of 77
Le Manif Pour Tous 103
Lerner, Max 81, 82
LGBTQ rights 35; Canada 37, 39
liberal-capitalism, communism *vs.* 13
liberalism 13
liberty 56–57
Liebman, Joshua Loth 101
Locke, John 80
Loewenstein, Rudolph 100
Lost Generation writers 76

Machine in the Garden (Marx) 84–85
Maier, Thomas 94–95

Malaquais, Jean 82
Mandela, Nelson 22
Manning, Preston 54, 58–59
market freedom, Reform Party (Canada) 61–62
marriage equality *see* same-sex marriage/marriage
equality
Marx, Leo 71, 74, 80, 84–85
Massive Open Online Course (MOOC) 4,
9–26; analysis 11; community *see* community;
freedom *see* freedom; justice *see* justice;
political ideas 11; *see also* crowd-sourced
political ideas
Matthiessen, F. O. 6, 70–71; American studies
movement 73, 74; Salzburg Seminar in
American Studies 71–72; un-American
classification 72; US cultural nation
building 73–74
Mazower, Mark 95
McCarthy, Mary 83
Melton, Andrew 54
Mencken, H. L. 81
Miller, Perry 76
minority rights, Reform Party (Canada)
opposition 59
Montessori, Maria 90
MOOC *see* Massive Open Online Course (MOOC)
Moore, G. E. 94
Moral Majority 35
morphological approach, Freeden *see* Freeden's
morphological approach
Moscovici, Sergei 101
Mouvement de Libération des Femmes 102
Mulroney, Brian 31, 38
Multiple Streams analysis 41–42
multi-symbol analysis 6
mutual influences, ideology studies 48

national borders, community 20
national communities 23
national culture, past *vs.* future 83–86
national governments, community 20
national identity, community 19
national independence, freedom as 14
nations, centred notion of 76–77
Native Son (Wright) 83–84
negative freedom 14
negroes *see* African-American civil rights
Neuhaus, Jogn 34
new nationalism (USA) 75
Nixon, Richard 33
non-elected representation 49
non-specialist discourse, crowd-sourced political
ideas 11–13
Norquist, Grover 46, 61
North America; conservatism, Freeden's
morphological approach 5; populist politics
46–69; social conservatism 27–45; *see also*
Canada; United States of America (USA)
nuclear family 95

On Native Grounds (Kazin) 76
over-determined representational/ideological
   practice 53

Palin, Sarah 36
Parsons, Talcott 76
Partisan Review (PR) 77–78
Peace of Mind (Liebman) 101
peripheral concepts, ideology studies 48
Pernoud, Laurence 96
personal experience, justice 18
personalisation of politics 21–24
Phillips, Howard 58
physical conflict, justice 17–18
Pichon, Édouard 99
Pinard, Adolphe 99
political iconographies 16–17
political ideas: freedom as 15–16; ideology and
   2–3; MOOC 11
political parties, freedom and 15–16
political regimes, justice 17–18
political representation, constructivist
   theorization (Saward) 63
political speech intensification, Freeden 52
political texts, context, effects of 2
politics: behaviours, effects of ideas 2; conflict
   in populist framing 51; freedom and 15–16;
   personalisation of 21–24; psychoanalysis
   98–99, 101
populism 5–6, 52–53
populist politics: conceptual foundations
   48; critiques of failed representation 47;
   elite-captured representations 49; Freeden/
   Saward hybrid approach 49–54; North
   America 46–69
The Portable Faulkner (Cowley) 76
positive freedom 14
post-war justice 18
post-war welfare state 29
preformative speech acts 51
Progressive Conservative Party (Canada) 39
Propaganda and Ideology in Everyday Life 9–26;
   see also crowd-sourced political ideas; Massive
   Open Online Course (MOOC)
Proposition 13 51; anti-statist understanding of
   liberty 56–57; Jarvis 54–58; opponents of
   55–56; result of 58
Prost, Antoine 92
Pro-Women Pro-Life 38
psychoanalysis: child development 103–104;
   child-rearing 6–7; child-rearing advice 89, 93,
   95–96, 101; Dolto 98; France 101–102; political
   connotations 98–99, 101
public intellectuals 3, 6
Pyke, Geoffrey 91

Rahv, Philip 82–83
Rankin, John E. 78–79
Rawls, John 30

Reagan, Ronald 31, 34–35; fusionist conservatives
   33–34; leadership ascent 58; tax reforms 54; tax
   revolts 46
REAL (Realistic, Equal, Active, for Life)
   Women 37–38
Reed, Ralph 35
Reform Party (Canada) 39, 51, 58–63; abortion
   61; Charlottetown Accord and 59; direct
   democracy 61; equality definition 62; minority
   rights, opposition to 59; negative publicity used
   59; re-branding 62–63; tax fairness 59; *see also*
   Canadian Conservative and Reform Alliance
relational process philosophy 77
religion: adherence in Canada 36–37;
   commitments in social conservatism 30;
   community 19; sentiment in USA 34
representation: elected/non-elected forms 49;
   legitimacy questioning 50–51
representative claim 5; general form of (Saward) 49
Republican party, fusionist conservatives and 33
Riesman, David 79, 82
rights of the child, Dolto 102–103
Robcis, Camille 103
Roe v. Wade 30, 33–34

Salzburg Seminar in American Studies,
   Matthiessen 71–72
same-sex marriage/marriage equality: Canada 37,
   39, 40; USA 35
Saward, Michael 47; constructivist theorization of
   political representation 53, 63; representative
   claim toolkit 49; shape-shifting model 52, 53
scapegoating 23–24
Schafley, Phyllis 34
Scheer, Andrew 40
Schiff, Paul 100
Schwartz, Delmore 83
The Second Sex (de Beauvoir) 101
self-authentication, communities 21
sense of self, lived experience and 3
sexology, French child-rearing 100
sexual revolution, USA 34
shape-shifting model, Saward 52, 53
Sharland, Elaine 91
Shorter, Edward 92
Smith, Henry Nash 71
smoking, freedom and 14–15
social changes, 1960s 28–29
social conservatism 28; Canada 36–41; definition
   28–31, 41; development 32; emergence 30–31;
   North America 27–45; USA 32–36
social engineering, Spock 94
social issues, traditionalists 30
social learners 10
social liberation, US Protestants 34
social order, social conservatism 29
society, centred notion of 76–77
special interests, definition by Reform Party
   (Canada) 60

Spock, Benjamin 6, 89–90, 91, 93; attack on 95–96; democracy and 94–95; social engineering 94
Stanfield, Robert 30, 38
St Aubyn, Gwen 91–92
Stearns, Harold 76
Steinem, Gloria 95–96
Summers, Hatton W. 78

tax fairness, Reform Party (Canada) 60–61
tax reforms: Canada 58–63; structure and strategy 47; voters, appeals to 63–64
tax revolts: direct democracy 54; North America 46–69
Taylor, Charles 12
This Sex Which Is Not One (Irigaray) 102
Thomson, Mathew 92
totalitarian ideology, child-rearing advice 93
traditionalism 28; eclipse of 29; social issues 30
Trilling, Lionel 81–82
Trump, Donald: "African carnage" inaugural address 51; "defend the defenceless" 50; election 2, 24; social conservatism 36; tax revolts 46; voice of the people as 64

United Organization of Taxpayers 55–56
United States of America (USA): 1968 elections 33; 1980 elections 33–34; anti-Soviet role 82–83; Canada, influence on 40–41; child-rearing advice 91–96; Constitution, Equal Rights Amendment to 33–34, 35; cultural nation building 73–78; direct democracy 54–58; ideology of Americanism 85–86; individualism 79; new nationalism 75; sense of belonging, Matthiessen 71; social conservatism 32–36
Urwin, Cathy 91

Vico, Giambattista 6, 73
Vigeurie, Richard 34

Wallace, Henry 77
Watson, John B. 91
Whitehead, Alfred North 77
Whitman, Walt 85
Wilcot, Donald 93
Williams, Raymond 76
Wolfendon report (UK) 38
Wright Mills, C. 73, 82
Wright, Richard 83–84

Zachry, Caroline B. 94
Zaretsky, Eli 92